The East & East Midlands

Edited by Donna Samworth

First published in Great Britain in 2009 by

 Young**Writers**

Remus House
Coltsfoot Drive
Peterborough
PE2 9JX
Telephone: 01733 890066
Website: www.youngwriters.co.uk

Foreword

At Young Writers our defining aim is to promote an enjoyment of reading and writing amongst children and young adults. By giving aspiring poets the opportunity to see their work in print, their love of the written word as well as confidence in their own abilities has the chance to blossom.

Our latest competition Poetry Explorers was designed to introduce primary school children to the wonders of creative expression. They were given free reign to write on any theme and in any style, thus encouraging them to use and explore a variety of different poetic forms.

We are proud to present the resulting collection of regional anthologies which are an excellent showcase of young writing talent. With such a diverse range of entries received, the selection process was difficult yet very rewarding. From comical rhymes to poignant verses, there is plenty to entertain and inspire within these pages. We hope you agree that this collection bursting with imagination is one to treasure.

Contents

Kensington Junior School, Ilkeston

Loscoe CE Primary School, Heanor

Manor House School, Ashby-de-la-Zouch

Mapperley Primary School, Mapperley Village

Millfield Primary School, North Walsham

Rothersthorpe CE Primary School, Northampton

St Botolph's CE Primary School, Peterborough

St Nicholas House School, North Walsham

St Winefride's Catholic Primary School, Shepshed

Sacred Heart Catholic School, Loughborough

Scalford CE Primary School, Melton Mowbray

Stanwick CP School, Wellingborough

The Grange School, Daventry

Viscount Beaumonts CE Primary School, Coalville

Waltham on the Wolds CE Primary School

The Poems

The Chase In Space

There once was a chase,
In the middle of space,
Near the Apollo base,
I saw a troll's face.
Tripped over my lace,
At a dangerous pace
In this draining race.

There came a man
Called Peter Pan.
Who'd met a man
Called Jackie Chan!

Once I got home,
I brought out my comb!
With plenty of foam,
In the winter dome,
Where I have come to roam.

I saw a flower,
As dull as Joseph Bower,
Needs a good shower,
And has no power!

In this town,
I bought a dressing gown!
Which turned my frown
Upside down!

Alex Nicholas Hewison (10)
Barlborough Primary School, Chesterfield

A Woman From Leeds

A woman from Leeds
Swallowed half a pack of seeds,
In less than an hour,
She turned into a flower
And her garden was full of weeds!

Vinnie Froggatt (11)
Barlborough Primary School, Chesterfield

Great Aunt Betty!

Dearest Great Aunt Betty,
The love of my love life.
Yesterday she threatened me,
With a carving knife!

She says I am too lazy,
She thinks I am a grouch.
When I picked her a daisy,
She left me on the couch!

I know she likes me lots and lots,
Even though she hits me.
So I washed her the dirty pots,
I really hoped she would kiss me.

But that starry night,
She went out to the pub.
So I was left,
In the learning hub.

She left me lying
On the floor,
So I was saying,
'Don't go, give me more!'

I had to find her,
I looked everywhere,
Upstairs, downstairs,
Even at the fair.

Eventually,
I found her alone.
She was drunk on the street,
So I took her home.

So now I think,
I must come to an end.
Cos all this writing's
Driving me round the bend!

Dearest Great Aunt Betty,
I do love you so.
Let's watch the programme, EastEnders,
Because it's your favourite show!

Charlotte Bushell (10)
Barlborough Primary School, Chesterfield

The 8 Times Table Song

I've got a friend whose name is Kate
8 x 1 that makes 8
My friend Kate met the Queen
2 x 8 makes 16
My friend Kate is at the door
3 x 8 makes 24
My friend Kate had swine flu
4 x 8 makes 32
My friend Kate is sometimes naughty
5 x 8 that makes 40
My friend Kate is at the gate
6 x 8 makes 48
My friend Kate is good at tricks
7 x 8 makes 56
My friend Kate mopped the floor
8 x 8 makes 64
My friend Kate went to the zoo
9 x 8 makes 72
My friend Kate is my best matey
10 x 8 that makes 80
My friend Kate is always late
11 x 8 makes 88
My friend Kate ate a Twix
12 x 8 makes 96.

Jack Ezard (10)
Barlborough Primary School, Chesterfield

3

Monster!

Hairy feet,
Awful to meet!
Red eyes,
Which attract flies.
Eggy smell
Does that ring a bell?

Malted fur,
Do you want to know more about her?
Pierced nose,
The smell flows.
Sticky hair,
Do you know it looks like a bear?

Loud footsteps,
Up the steep steps.
Yellow teeth,
She lives in a reef,
Huge ears
That's not the worst of your fears.
Long, stained nails.
Plus the constant wails.

You don't want to meet her on the street!

Annalise Guild (11)
Barlborough Primary School, Chesterfield

Up, Down, Around

There was a spider who went up the drain,
Down the drain and around the drain.

He goes up my arm, down my arm and around my arm.

He goes up the bath, down the bath and around the bath.

He goes up the web, down the web and around the web.

This spider goes up, down and around.

Jessica Jarvis (10)
Barlborough Primary School, Chesterfield

Animals' Picnic

I'm at the animals' picnic,
And all that I can see,
Animals, animals, animals,
And they are all staring at me!

Elephants as big as houses,
Ducks as small as stones,
Mice not much bigger than a pebble,
And a rat that is baking some scones.

I'm at the animals' picnic,
And all that I can see,
Animals, animals, animals,
And they are all staring at me!

Birds tweeting softly,
Penguins waddling around,
Bears are all roaring,
Bees hovering over the ground.

The animals love their picnic,
The keepers do too,
The people just keep clapping,
They want to join in too!

Fallon Smith-Kerry (10)
Barlborough Primary School, Chesterfield

The Strange Thing

The strange thing walked round and round,
His quiet footsteps not making a sound.

The spines on his back looked very prickly,
His arms were long and incredibly tickly.

His tongue hung out liked chewed paper,
He wore the hat of a waiter.

His eyes on his head were very few,
As a matter of fact, he had only two!

The teeth in his mouth were very scary,
His ears were large and immensely hairy!

His feet were pink, green and black,
He carried a rucksack on his back.

He had great big bogeys up his nose,
He had millions of warts all over his toes!

He snuck into the room without a hoot . . .

'Oh Daddy,' said Millie, 'that's a silly Hallowe'en suit!'

Emily Tinsley (11)
Barlborough Primary School, Chesterfield

Ponies Everywhere!

Ponies in a field,
Running around everywhere,
Just like they don't care.

Cantering and galloping, having fun,
Leaping and jumping in the morning sun.

Grazing on the green,
Bucking and rearing as they gleam,
Thinking of nothing as they dream.

Cantering and galloping, having fun,
Leaping and jumping in the morning sun.

Sarah Elizabeth Bache (9)
Barlborough Primary School, Chesterfield

Bob The Alien

There once was an alien called Bob,
Who lived on the planet Zog,
It was always covered in fog
And he had a pet dog.

He ate children's mums
And he loved biting their bums!
The children were so grateful,
They gave him plateful after plateful!

Bob liked to live in the woods
Because then he could get a few goods,
He especially enjoyed a rat
And it made him really fat!

Even though Bob was from Zog,
Which had a really bad fog,
Earth was the place for him,
And he never became slim!

George Hilditch (10)
Barlborough Primary School, Chesterfield

Flowers In Springtime

The flowers in springtime blooming pleasantly,
Whilst the super, shimmering sun beats down,
The insects flutter by, they can smell the smell of sweet nectar,
They lick and eat it while the pollen sticks to them.

Flowers in springtime,

The colours of their petals are distinguished
And not to mention the smell of them when they tickle your nose.
While the super shimmering sun beats down,
The flowers bloom delightfully,
All in one garden there's daffodils and bluebells,
And the odd leaping Lilly.

All on one super sunny day.

Molly Beth Hemsworth Watson (10)
Barlborough Primary School, Chesterfield

7

Super Gran

As quick as a wink she ran through town,
Her green eyes sparkled like jewels in a crown.
The robbers were catching up fast,
A superhero is how she is classed.
What she does is truly amazing,
By now the robber's eyes were blazing!
Her purple cape blew in the wind,
Her grey hair became unpinned.

She turned a corner, towards the rubbish bins,
That is where she hides - she always wins.
With the purse in one hand and the bag of swag in the other,
She swung open the door which made some people shudder!
'It is I, Super Gran!' she shouted across the room,
Everybody cheered and it broke up the gloom.
She pulled off her trainers and ripped off her mask,
Another good deed, finished at last!

Harriet Lunn (10)
Barlborough Primary School, Chesterfield

Random

Random Brandon went to bed,
But he saw drop dead Fred,
He ran and ran in glee,
Screaming back, 'The world's fattest hippo and me!'
He pegged it fast to the abbey,
Looking for Mr Shabbey,
He said, 'I should see him mum because she had a cream bun,'
I ate the bun, it made me feel bloated,
If it wasn't for the sun, I would have floated!
I drank lemonade the next day,
It made me say hip hip hooray.
Now we are at the end,
Random Brandon is off to spend!

Mitchell Billyeald (11)
Barlborough Primary School, Chesterfield

Great Golf

You walk up to the tee,
To see the lush green fairways and me.
The trees are bright and green,
With colourful leaves and the sky,
Shines bright at night with no fright!

You pick up your club with great thought,
And then realise the sport is harder than it looks.

The small, white golf ball soars high up in the sky,
Then soon it falls down with a crash!

The lakes are bright blue which surround the green,
And if you look around it, it is really quite a sight,
I think the clubhouse doesn't look good pink.

But it is great if you have a drink!
(But not if you are young!)

Thomas Lodge (11)
Barlborough Primary School, Chesterfield

Strange

There once was Zog,
From the planet, Pog,
Who had a very strange day.
His dad, Mr God,
Turned into a log
And rolled out into the bay.
His mum Mrs Boo,
Ran out there too,
Hoping that he was OK!

Then there was the sound
Of the barking space hound,
Who pulled them back intact.
Everyone was alright,
Although white with fright,
Which is a matter of fact!

Adam Cunliffe (11)
Barlborough Primary School, Chesterfield

The Boy

There was a boy called Ben,
Who hung out in his den,
With his best mate Dick,
Who was very thick.

Then Ben's mum came,
Who was called Jane.
Jane had a big pot,
Which was very hot.

Jane went away,
Because she had to pay,
To get inside,
Or she would have had to hide.

Ben was fine,
So Dick had some wine.

Matthew James Hale (10)
Barlborough Primary School, Chesterfield

Shopping!

Shops over here,
Shops over there,
Shops everywhere.

One shop, two shop,
Three shop, four shop,
How many clothes can you buy with £1.34?
About one shoe, how about you?

Primark, Tammy Girl,
New Look and Next,
How about a pair of earrings from Claire's?

Maybe some leg warmers from Next.

Ellie Louise Marshall (9)
Barlborough Primary School, Chesterfield

Fabulous Friends

Friends, friends, they're the best thing in life,
They'll keep you going all day and night,
They stand by you no matter what,
They make you smile a lot,
They will come to your parties no matter where or when
And sometimes in lessons they'll lend you a pen,
They care about you when you're down,
So you should turn your frown upside down,
So don't give up on your friends because
They will be there until the end!

Charlotte Carter (10)
Barlborough Primary School, Chesterfield

Happy Hippos!

Hippos are big, hippos are fat,
They like to roll around in the mud that's flat,
When they've been wallowing in the mud,
The sun shines down and makes them red,
However, this makes them lazy,
So they doze off to bed,
When they awake, they give a big yawn,
Their teeth are quite large but never too small,
The mud on their backs has dried to a crisp,
Which makes them feel as cool as the mist!

Kayleigh Dunn (11)
Barlborough Primary School, Chesterfield

The Man

There was once a man from Brigg,
Who ate his tea like a pig,
When he sat down to eat up his peas,
He always had an attishoo sneeze!

Matthew Tindall (9)
Baslow St Anne's CE School, Bakewell

The Sun Breaks

The sun breaks,
Through forgotten clouds,
The light creates,
Without a sound.

The eagle soars,
Through the sky,
The wind ignores
And passes by.

Light reflects,
Off beady eyes,
The dark neglects,
Where sunbeams glide.

The trees look up,
To admire,
Leaves dry up
And expire.

Clouds drift back,
Regaining power,
The lightning cracks,
That starts the shower.

The raindrops fall,
A soothing sound,
More and more,
Falls down, down, down.

Immersing nature,
Rain revives,
Sunbeams traitor,
Again life thrives.

Freddie Ostrovskis (11)
Baslow St Anne's CE School, Bakewell

My Teacher's Socks

Miss Care has lots of socks
Some are pink and some are frilly
Some have spots and some have stripes
Some have bells and some have jewels
Some are big and some are small.

Miss Care has named them all
One's called John and one's called Bob
One's called Cutie and one's called Pie
One's called Ron and one's called Jean
One's called Anna and one's called Beanie.

One's dressed as a twirling genie
One's dressed as a big fat pig
One's dressed up as a big brown book
One's dressed as a dazzling prince
One's dressed up as a scary punk.

Some smell of a smelly skunk
Some smell of stinky cheese
Some smell of lovely roses
Some smell of down the loo.

Miss Care has got the lot.

Jessica Wilgose (10)
Baslow St Anne's CE School, Bakewell

If I Were . . .

If I were an astronaut,
What a sight to see,
Flying up around the moon,
Then be back in time for tea.

If I were a fisherman,
Way out at sea,
I'd race around to catch the tide,
A sailor's life for me.

If I were an explorer,
I'd find a mummy's tomb,
I'd creep across the dusty floor,
While scary shadows loom.

But I'm just a kid,
That's just me,
I'm not around the stars,
In a tomb or at sea.

I'd rather just ride horses,
Or climb a massive tree,
Or swing around on monkey bars,
Or sit and watch TV.

Gabrielle Wickersham (10)
Baslow St Anne's CE School, Bakewell

One Little . . .

One little bee,
That will sting me.
One little horse,
Covered in sauce.
One little fruit fly,
Making me sigh.
One little monkey,
Making me funky.
One little dragon,
Sitting in a wagon.
One little panda,
Staring at Amanda.
One little whale,
Making bread stale.
One little fish,
Giving me a wish.
One little otter,
Who likes Harry Potter.
One little bee,
That's what I see.

Ellie Anderson (9)
Baslow St Anne's CE School, Bakewell

My Superstar Sister

She wears a red sparkly dress,
She's sweet and neat and never a mess,
She can sing and dance,
She can do what she wants,
She has 21 boyfriends who love her a lot,
She's in all the mags,
Always looks pretty and never wears rags,
It's odd having her as a sister,
When she's away I always miss her,
But the most odd thing is she's only three,
But I'll love her forever my sister and me.

Lisa Dwyer-Joyce (10)
Baslow St Anne's CE School, Bakewell

Om, Om, Om

Om, om, om

Where's that sound coming from I wonder?
It doesn't sound like rain or wind or thunder.

Om, om, om

It could be a cat or the creaky floor,
Or maybe it could be the rickety door.

Om, om, om

I can hear a strange sound but I don't know what it is,
I go and check on Sanjay but it is not him.

Om, om, om

Oh I know, it could be Dad snoring,
Or it could be the tree in the wind groaning.

Om, om, om

I go to look outside but it is not the tree,
I look a little lower and I see Grandpa Chatterji!

Oscar Thomas Oliver Baldwin & Harry Poole (9)
Baslow St Anne's CE School, Bakewell

My Mum's A Superhero

Most mums are gentle, kind and sweet,
They like to look pretty, and tidy and neat.
But most mums are like that, they make such a fuss,
Even when you're in trouble, and you miss the school bus.
My mum's not like that, oh no she is not,
She can fly, she can sing, she can dance quite a lot.
She's been many places, to Egypt and Rome,
And she always has a tan, when she comes home.
So there you have it, my mum's as neat as a big, fat zero,
But what you must know, is she's a superhero!

Louise Maynard-Singh (10)
Baslow St Anne's CE School, Bakewell

Ronald Eats Too Many Sweets!

Ronald eats too many sweets
And he has cheesy, smelly feet,
His armpits smell like rotten meat,
Ronald eats too many sweets.

Humbugs, lollipops, gobstoppers, everything,
When he gives his friends a ring,
He's always chewing, chewing, chewing,
He's a sweet king.

Ronald eats too many sweets,
He's obviously very fat
And his face looks like a rat,
He has a very long nose
And ginormous eyes
And did I not mention that he has a lot of sweet blueberry pies?
Ronald eats too many sweets.

Anna Esmé Cairns (10)
Baslow St Anne's CE School, Bakewell

Ten Things In My Magical Box

A super-duper-truper-tabyfastic word,
A glittery, violet, dancing outfit that can change
Its fashionable style,
A ring tone on my brand new mobile,
A scrumdelicious mix of fizzy drinks,
Full to the brim, always refilling with a different flavour.
A changing colour make-up set
That tells you what to wear with your outfit,
A midday, when the sun is gleaming on your back,
Scorching and shining too bright to miss it.
A young Capibara that can speak any language,
A selection of delectable sweets that are everlasting,
A microphone that can play the violin,
A book that never runs out of pages.

Sara Goodban (10)
Christ Church CE Primary School, Chesterfield

If I Ruled The World

Ban school, and change it into a golf course,
Vegetables cancelled, just junk food, of course,
Almost everything is free,
Play St Andrews for 2p,
Definitely keep the European Tour,
Tap a putt in for a four,
Ban smoking,
Make it impossible to get hurt,
You can roll about in the dirt
Make more golf courses,
Tapton Park golf club will hold The Open,
Even though it is not a links,
The green jacket would become even more famous,
I would give Sheffield United Football club
£150m to spend on Kaka, Ronaldo or even Messi!
David Leadbetter would be my personal golf coach.
Would you like it?
What a life!

Sam Barker-Sabido (10)
Christ Church CE Primary School, Chesterfield

If I Ruled The World . . .

I would look after every pet and animal,
I would do more history and maths and PE,
I would play all day,
I would be helpful,
I would go to every theme park in the world,
I would be rich,
I would swim,
I would have a chocolate room,
I would ride my horse every day,
I would have the best bed in the world,
I would have everything I wanted,
I would have the nicest dresses in the world.

PS. I would live on a ship sometimes.

Katie Hopkinson
Christ Church CE Primary School, Chesterfield

If I Ruled The World!

If I ruled the world,
I would be the manager of Liverpool Football Club
And make them the best team in the world,
I would make up my own football song about me,
I would ban money forever so everything was free,
Green vegetables banned because I think you should just eat
Carrots, peas and beans!
Turn every single field into a football pitch,
No school, I would only allow school for one day
But you only have to do fun stuff,
Make rubbish football teams play international teams,
That would be awesome!
Chesterfield vs Brazil,
That one day when you go to school, you get paid,
All houses made of chocolate,
And finally cars that can fly,
I'm not asking for much am I?

Thomas Rowland (10)
Christ Church CE Primary School, Chesterfield

Sophie's Box Of Magic

Well what would I find in my magic box?

The words of the best football team:
Liverpool, 'You'll Never Walk Alone,'
A mouth-watering chocolate cake,
Leaking with chocolate moss,
A glass full of fizzy Coke,
Noisy bells ringing in the distance,
A football that reflates itself,
Rainbow coloured shoes,
A talking football that tells you what football boots to wear,
Midday when I can play football with my friends,
A mirror that talks,
And the cutest cat ever.

Sophie Jane Law (10)
Christ Church CE Primary School, Chesterfield

If I Ruled The World . . .

If I ruled the world, let me see, I would . . .

Have a cute puppy,
Let celebrities visit the town and sing with them,
Get most things for free like food, clothes, pets, maybe a hen,
And, of course, with me, you would not have to go to boring school,
You could stay at home and be cool,
I would make small houses into mansions,
Make you wear every new fashion,
Ban smoking altogether,
So we can be healthy forever,
Get every style of food, in every city,
And serve them to me,
Wear a ballgown like a princess,
Have a posh accent instead of, 'Yeah,' say 'Yes'.
Get cinema tickets for 10p, they will never get sold,
This would happen if I ruled the world.

Anisa Ali (11)
Christ Church CE Primary School, Chesterfield

What Is In My Magic Box?

In my magic box there is a glass of pink milkshake
That bubbles in your mouth.

A rabbit sniffing in the background.

A pair of sparkling shoes you can never get rid of.

Floating on the dance floor in a pink silky dress.

A plate full of tuna pasta that you can eat forever.

A really sunny day that lasts all day.

Friends forever, will always be.

Getting cute rabbits out to hold.

Drawing pictures all day long.

Abbie Lindley (9)
Christ Church CE Primary School, Chesterfield

If I Ruled The World

I would ban school altogether
And make it a football ground
So children can play better,
Make houses into mansions
With the latest fashion,
Make younger brothers and sisters
Your servants if they're annoying,
Because they're boring,
Get paid to go to school,
If you do, you'll be cool,
Go to school when you want,
So you can go on XBox Live,
And that's what I'd do if I ruled the world!

Shannon Dinnen (11)
Christ Church CE Primary School, Chesterfield

If I Ruled The World . . .

I'd make everything under 50p,
I'd have a super duper pink singing rabbit,
I'd make every holiday under £2,
I'd have a brilliant blue ferret that gets me what I want,
I'd only go to school when I want,
So I can relax,
I'd have whatever I want for tea and dinner,
I'd have a fabulous football that changes colour when you kick it,
I'd give older people more money,
I'd have my favourite songs on my MP3 to sing and sing along to,
I'd have a microphone that would make my voice brilliant,
Servants all day, that would be my mum and dad!
Do you like it?

Hannah Jade Williams (10)
Christ Church CE Primary School, Chesterfield

Ten Things In My Magic Box

A mouth-watering raspberry,
A delicious strawberry milkshake that never runs out,
Mary Poppins' wonderful purple suitcase bursting with surprises,
A rainbow skipping rope that changes into different objects,
A chubby rabbit that never stops eating,
A world that no one can think of,
When the clock strikes 12pm at lunch,
Black as night leggings that are so warm,
A bill from the pet shop,
A gorgeous guinea pig squeaking.

Are you getting a magic box now?
They're from Tesco.

Charlotte Minor (10)
Christ Church CE Primary School, Chesterfield

What Can You Find In My Magic Box?

Bubbling milkshake that refills each time I drink it.

Pulling out a giant hill for me so I can climb to the top
And back roll down, over and over again.

Silky as a feather and as fluffy as a pillow,
The cute small kitten that lies there, softly miaows a song.

I love to eat marble cake that once I have eaten it,
It cooks itself into a different two flavours each time.

I found a pot at the end of my rainbow,
But by the time I looked in, there was only one penny left.

What is in your magic box?

Eloise Elizabeth Bestwick (10)
Christ Church CE Primary School, Chesterfield

9 Things Found In My Magic Box

These are the things found in my box.

A strawberry milkshake filled to the top,
And a chocolate bar that never ever stops,
A cuddly teddy which I almost forgot,
And a skipping rope tied in a knot,
A cute dog which I love a lot,
And a lovely top that I wear when it's hot,
My favourite room full of polka dots,
A dish full of yummy hot pot,
My best thing in the box is a bag of Jelly Tots.

These are the things found in my magic box!

Emma Harding (11)
Christ Church CE Primary School, Chesterfield

Ten Things In A Magic Box

A fizzy Diet Coke that refills always when you give it chocolate,
A squealing, pink, fuzzy pig eating pizza and ice cream,
Being football crazy for the football world,
A Man Utd top signed by mega Ronaldo,
White chocolate that changes colour with every bite,
The invincible words 'Man Utd till I die,'
A crazy zapping frog,
A monkey as a butler,
A midsummer's day sitting in the blazing hot sun,
Having Christmas every day.

A very merry everyday Christmas everyone.

Nathan Moorcroft
Christ Church CE Primary School, Chesterfield

Ten Things In My Magic Box!

Fizzy shandy that quenches my thirst,
Juicy, sweet and sour, slipping down my throat,
A Koenigsegg speeding around my body,
A huge dog that talks all day,
Courageous football crowds cheering for me,
Some magic football boots that make you score,
Blazing hot sun at midday,
A gigantic bill from Pizza Hut,
A pair of trainers that make you fly,
An invisible microphone that makes me sing better!

That's what is in my magic box, would you like it?

Joshua Brearley (11)
Christ Church CE Primary School, Chesterfield

If I Ruled The World

If I ruled the world
I would watch TV every day.

I would have lots of money,
I would own my own chocolate factory,
I would go swimming every day,
I would never go to bed at night,
I would have a house made out of chocolate,
I would go to every after school club,
I would have a purple dress to float around on the floor,
I would have a skirt,
Plus take my place and buy a ticket to Laserland.

Bryony Collier (8)
Christ Church CE Primary School, Chesterfield

Nine Things Found In My Magic Box

A morning sky, bright and sunny,
A nice soft shirt,
Ice-cold Pepsi that never empties,
A cuddly cat that changes colour,
Barks of a hound, *woof, woof, woof,*
Slithering silver snakes,
Some nice soft cakes with springy sponge,
A group of flutes playing a harmony,
And a little cap of leaves, only if you say please!
All of these things are found in my magic box,
My box is unbelievable!

David Charles Clewett (10)
Christ Church CE Primary School, Chesterfield

What's In My Magic Box?

What's in my magic box?
The word love, to cuddle when I'm upset,
A flipback T-shirt, since it's summer,
A blackbird's song which flows in and out,
Lacto-free milk, so lovely and creamy,
A box to hide in, very amusing,
In the evening, my favourite time,
The talent of painting, very exciting,
A bowl of Miso soup, yummy!
And a purring cat, sitting on a chair,
That's the top nine things to put in a magic box.

Jesse Robinson (8)
Christ Church CE Primary School, Chesterfield

 YoungWriters

If I Ruled The World

I would . . .
Have a palace made out of chocolate,
A supercar that can fly,
No school,
Make every single thing in the world free,
Live off Coke, crisps and cake,
Have a monkey as a butler,
Go to sleep whenever you want,
Have Christmas every day of the year,
A time machine that can travel back in time,
Where would you go?

Luke Boden (10)
Christ Church CE Primary School, Chesterfield

Ten Things Found In My Magical Box

A light blue denim jacket to keep the cold out,
A blazing hot day for me to keep warm,
A nasty car engine that chugs all day every day,
An abracazap to make my cake grow,
A colourful milkshake that changes colour with every sip,
A black and white massive cow,
A multi-coloured skipping rope that flashes every jump,
A dark pink flying pig,
A thick beef sandwich that changes flavour every bite,
A huge chocolate bar that changes every taste.

Sarah-Jane Collier (10)
Christ Church CE Primary School, Chesterfield

If I Ruled The World!

If I ruled the world, I would free all animals from the zoo,
I would burn all the schools in the world
And everything would be free,
I would let kids go in the Army and make hunting stop forever,
I would also put Chesterfield in the Premier League
And stop smoking,
And everyone would live in a mansion,
Including people on the streets,
And no one would have to pay bills,
I'm not asking for much, am I?

Lewis Hooper (11)
Christ Church CE Primary School, Chesterfield

What Is In My Magic Box?

In my magic box there is a pair of old jeans,
The sound of classical music playing in the background,
A nice cosy word which is warmth,
A refreshing glass of milk, nice and creamy,
A big bowl of tasty pasta waiting for me,
My best time of day is a sunny afternoon,
A little rabbit, sniff, sniff, sniffing,
A pair of trainers you never grow out of,
A writing book full of my stories,
Now you know what is in my magic box.

Rose Stone (9)
Christ Church CE Primary School, Chesterfield

Five Things In My Magic Box!

Mouth-watering milkshake,
Always refills with a different flavour every time I drink it.
A fantastic footballer zooming down the pitch to keep him fit.
Delicious pasta hopping into my mouth.
A courageous football crowd heading south.
A cute dog barking to go for a walk in the fog.

Alfie Spencer (10)
Christ Church CE Primary School, Chesterfield

If I Ruled The World . . .

If I ruled the world, I would make crisps and chocolate
A healthy diet instead of salad and fruit.

I would ban school and make a law that everyone must
Love rock concerts and go to one every night.

I would make a law that all animals must be cared for properly.

I would be the most famous person in the world.

And last, but definitely not least,
I would make the world a better place.

Emily Davies (8)
Christ Church CE Primary School, Chesterfield

If I Ruled The World

If I ruled the world . . .

I would lay in bed all day and eat chocolate,
I would care for all the animals in the world,
I would go to Alton Towers for free,
I would be a professional singer,
I would own the Queen's palace and be a princess,
I would get all the swimming pools and put them in my back garden.
I would get everything I like for free,
I would get a table of my very own.

Lauren Hooper (9)
Christ Church CE Primary School, Chesterfield

If I Ruled The World . . .

I would . . .

Have a palace made out of chocolate,
Ban school altogether,
Get a super car that can fly up into the sky,
Live off cold, fizzy cola, crisps and mouth-watering cake,
Have a time machine so I could travel into the future
To see what the lottery numbers are.

Benjamin Ragsdale (10)
Christ Church CE Primary School, Chesterfield

What Is In My Magic Box?

Laughter that goes on forever,
A violet dress to dance around a sparkling ballroom,
Blackbirds tweeting sweetly, to fill my ears with joy,
A bottle of fizzy Coke,
A dog that fills me with happiness,
Buckets of tiny little creatures that dazzle in the moonlight,
Chocolate that melts in your mouth,
The night that dazzles whilst the music goes on,
I have a shimmery silver piano that I am extremely good at playing.

Kayla Clarke (9)
Christ Church CE Primary School, Chesterfield

What Is In My Magic Box?

An evening at sunset when lights fade away,
A teddy that brings happiness all through the day,
A scarlet-red dress with roses and diamond petals,
A magic carpet that's like an aeroplane,
A glass of orange juice that's fizzy when shook,
A piano playing quietly in the background,
A pizza to eat when people get hungry,
A brown horse to ride in the country,
To show my talent, to ride all day in the country and far away.

Madison Swift (8)
Christ Church CE Primary School, Chesterfield

What Is In My Magic Box?

A hug when you pull it out of your pocket,
A top that has zebra patterns on,
A noise like a zebra,
A glass of lemonade that never runs out,
A magic wand that can help you magic things,
The best time of day for me is night,
An animal that is a puppy and a Dalmatian,
To eat, I choose a chocolate bar,
A talent would be looking after my dog.

Bobbi-Jo Skelton (7)
Christ Church CE Primary School, Chesterfield

What Is In My Magic Box?

A bucketful of shimmering stars,
Moons and clouds that mark a pathway to Mars,
A top made out of leopard skin and diamonds,
A pink piglet that never stops squealing,
A jug full of the dark night, that goes all the way round the world,
A word that nobody will ever spell for all of eternity,
A bag of chips that will never end,
A Ferrari car that will never run out of petrol,
A bike that can fly through the sky.

Thomas Key (8)
Christ Church CE Primary School, Chesterfield

What's In My Magic Box?

A word that only I shall ever know,
The beautiful sound of singing,
A dolphin the size of a purse,
Prawn cocktail crisps mixed with salt and vinegar crisps,
Lunchtime,
A glass of bubbling Fanta orange filled to the top,
A ten foot midnight-black trampoline,
A glittery red carpet for me to walk down,
A scarlet red dress spelling out my name in shimmering diamonds.

Charlie Nadin (8)
Christ Church CE Primary School, Chesterfield

Eight Things In My Magic Box

A super Arsenal shirt signed by Theo Walcott,
A Mini Cooper with sirens,
A pink football that never moves,
A wiggling worm that can wiggle to the centre of the Earth,
Greeting midday with the scorching, hot sun,
Black chocolate that changes flavour in every bite,
A crazy golf game that does not do any harm,
A Christmas cracker, cracking a Christmas surprise,
Well that's my magic box!

Kyle Martin (11)
Christ Church CE Primary School, Chesterfield

If I Ruled The World

I would get biscuits and chocolate all the time,
I would even knock schools down,
I would go out all the time,
I would care for all the animals in the world,
I would get a red Ferrari for free,
I would own a chocolate factory,
I would have the biggest swimming pool in the world,
I would leave all my clothes scattered about,
I would own everything.

Callum Billyeald (9)
Christ Church CE Primary School, Chesterfield

What Is In My Magic Box?

At sunset I would feel in my box,
And bring out the quiet, peaceful sound of birds singing,
I put in my box a knitted soft jumper,
A drink of water and a pile of pizzas,
Of course, I would not forget a pony to ride on later,
A piece of paper and paintbrush too,
A handkerchief the size of a car park,
Also a warm blanket to hug at night.

Rebecca Lomas (9)
Christ Church CE Primary School, Chesterfield

If I Ruled The World

I would rob banks,
I would play on games all day long,
I would knock down schools,
I would create a school that only teaches art,
I would have a big chocolate fountain in my back yard,
I would also have my own chocolate factory,
I would execute all the teaches except Miss Paterson,
I would go to all the theme parks in the world.

Brad King (8)
Christ Church CE Primary School, Chesterfield

School Memories

School, school, my first day,
All my freedom had gone away,
My best friends are Heather and Finlay,
When they first saw me they smiled dimly,
School, school,
In Year 1,
Proper lessons had begun,
My gloves were flushed down the loo,
By Courtney, Georgina and Natasha too,
School, school,
In Year 2,
My dream had come true,
We had this teacher called Mrs Cooper,
According to me she was super,
School, school,
In Year 3,
Chloe fell out with me,
We were talking about ourselves
She didn't like me 'cause I called her an elf,
School, school,
In Year 4,
Miss Wallace walked through the door,
We all thought she was very pretty,
But indeed she was very witty,
School, school,
In Year 5,
We learnt how to do the jive,
It was fun but I hurt my knee,
Not to mention I got stung by a bee,
School, school,
In Year 6,
I came in eating a Twix,
Strange it's my last year,
I think I'm going to miss it here.

Amy Moore (11)
Corby Old Village Primary School, Corby

My School Memories

I remember, I remember,
The third of September,
My first day of school.

Our great teacher,
Mrs Dredge,
A great person.

Mrs Cooper, Mrs Cooper,
Really, really, really super,
Sadly gone away,
But watching little angels play.

Miss Wallace, Miss Wallace,
Who fancies John Terry,
Can give you the stare
And be very, very scary.

Mrs Williams, Mrs Williams,
We've had you for two years,
When we leave,
I'm staying off the tears!

Mrs Hill, Mrs Hill,
Our best science teacher,
You taught us gases and forces too,
We'll be sad to see the back of you.

Finlay Cooney (11)
Corby Old Village Primary School, Corby

School Memories

I remember, I remember,
My first day of school,
I walked into the playground
And it looked really cool.

I said, 'It's OK Mummy, I'll be fine,'
Then I saw Amy from pre-school,
I shouted, 'Amy, look, it's me!'
Then she said, 'Hi, do they have a pool?'

Our teacher Mrs Dredge said, 'Come on girls,'
We followed her into the classroom,
In a world of whirls.

We listened to her as she said, 'Sit down.'
Then we said, 'OK'.
We went to school for ages and ages
And then we started a full day.

Now we've come to our senses,
We're in Year 6,
The SATs are coming up
And we're all in a mix.
School memories are the *best!*

Heather Phillips (11)
Corby Old Village Primary School, Corby

School Memories

I remember, I remember,
Mrs Williams was a nice person
And she was good at teaching,
She had short, grey hair
And she had a lovely smile,
She taught me lots of subtraction,
Which I needed for my SATs,
I will not meet a teacher like her again.

Natasha Brand (10)
Corby Old Village Primary School, Corby

School Memories

On the first day of school I remember
Breaking my arm in the middle of September,
When I got to hospital they put a plaster cast on
And then after a few months the plaster cast had gone.

I went to Hilltop in Year 3,
And from the dining room I could see the sea,
Some of the activities were at great heights,
When I was up there, I could see amazing sights.

In Year 4 I went to the Isle of Wight
And Georgina Dallimer came in the middle of the night,
We went to a museum, I was very scared!
Amy Moore almost fainted, (apart from me) no one really cared!

Now I am in Year 6,
It's getting near the end,
Soon I will have to say goodbye,
But I will always remember my friends!

I'd like to say a big thank you to Mrs Williams,
You were the best, I will never forget you!

Eve McIntyre (11)
Corby Old Village Primary School, Corby

My School Memories

I remember, I remember
My first day at school,
I didn't know anybody
And didn't like the rules.

I remember, I remember
Walking into the classroom,
The teacher was called Miss Wallace
And the thing I thought was doom.

I remember, I remember
My head teacher was Mrs Dredge,
She was very kind and funny,
I miss her so much,
She made my day all sunny.

I remember, I remember
My first day in Year 6,
I got really confused,
In a muddle and a mix.

Memories that remain.

Aimee Warrior (10)
Corby Old Village Primary School, Corby

My School Memories

On the first day of school,
I was very, very shy,
I saw all of the other children,
Waving as they passed by.

I made a friend called Amy,
She was really kind to me,
She helped me off the floor,
When I fell and grazed my knee.

And now I'm in Year 6,
I have made a friend called Eve,
It will be really sad,
When we all have to leave.

So there are a few
Of my school memories,
When I leave, I will cry,
So to everybody at Corby Old Village,
Thank you and goodbye!

Rachel Sheen (10)
Corby Old Village Primary School, Corby

I Remember!

I remember, I remember
My first day of school,
Lots of friends I nearly lost,
I flushed the gloves down the loo!

I remember, I remember
In Class 2,
When I had my first boyfriend,
He was quite a fool!

I remember, I remember
Our school talent show,
On stage with my fluffy dog,
Nerves, but who would know?

Courtney Rosetta Haggart (11)
Corby Old Village Primary School, Corby

My School Memories

I remember, I remember,
I didn't like the teacher,
Because of what she did to me,
She looked like a creature.

I remember, I remember,
My first day at school,
I was forced into my class,
I was made such a fool.

I remember, I remember,
I used to be scared of school,
I used to pretend I was ill,
But my mum had to stick to the rules.

I remember, I remember,
I really liked after school club,
I didn't like the activities,
I also hated the grub.

Georgina Reay (11)
Corby Old Village Primary School, Corby

The Hunted Hunter · Haikus

Rabbit
Rabbit ate the grass
And gazed up at the blue sky,
Basking in the sun.

Fox
Fox stalked through the grass,
She spied her unfortunate prey,
She pounced, tasted blood.

Hunter
The horn can be heard
And the bellowing of dogs,
They're getting closer.

Louise Penn (10)
Denton Primary School, Northampton

I Wonder

I wonder what happens to a bird,
The way it changes to a bird from a small egg,
Those streamlined wings that glide through the air,
As it brushes the leaves of tall, strong trees,
It soars through things that you would never imagine,
As it flaps its feathered wings,
Like a plane drifting through the air
And the only trace of the bird being here . . .
Is a feather lying on the ground.

Lewis Newton (11)
Denton Primary School, Northampton

A Shoot

Seeds sown, bulbs planted,
Roots grow earthbound,
Elegant blossom floating down,
Decorating the earthy ground.
Water droplets drift down,
Dampening the roots below,
What comes up?
A speck of green,
A shoot.

Molly Cronin (11)
Denton Primary School, Northampton

In The Vast Aged Oak Tree

In the vast aged oak tree,
Just over by the stream,
The large strong trunk, inhabited,
With fairies, tiny and bright.

Their coloured petal skirts
Flutter in the wind,
Drink dew from a bottle,
Listen to the stream.

Hannah Lidbetter (11)
Denton Primary School, Northampton

40

The Nest

I gazed into the moss-covered nest,
Hidden in the tall spring grass,
The beautiful tiny eggs were just in sight,
Of their small red-chested mother,
Her eyes glistened in the bright sun,
Her tail flittered,
I moved away,
She moved closer.

Giorgia Egan (11)
Denton Primary School, Northampton

The First Day Of Spring

I turned to see,
It was like another world,
It had birds with baby birds,
The tiny chicks were so fluffy.
The buds of all different colours,
The blossom smelt so floral.
It was sunny and warm, I felt so happy,
I felt glad to see them.

Chelsea Shellard (11)
Denton Primary School, Northampton

A Nest In Our School

The nest so rough and hard,
Up in the dark and gloomy trees,
With eggs and a proud mum
Sitting on the white, speckled eggs,
Waiting for them to hatch,
Wailing and waiting
Into the glazing night,
For the young chicks to hatch in the nest.

Ethan Wood (10)
Denton Primary School, Northampton

Tiny Wren

Tiny wren, tiny wren,
I'm glad to see you back again,
Now all the cold days have gone,
The cold day wren is here again.

Her soft wings spread as
She swoops into the trees,
There lies her rough nest.

Ellie Wood (10)
Denton Primary School, Northampton

Lush Spring

Lush green grass,
Which lambs leap over,
Seeds shooting out of the ground,
Baby birds squealing,
As their mothers feed them,
Morning dew dripping off the leaves,
Newly sprouted.

Ryan Shellard (11)
Denton Primary School, Northampton

The Robin Eggs

I find a dark hole,
Waiting for me to approach,
I stand there while the wind blows on my face,
Whistling right through my skull,
There in a tree, a pile of moss,
I peer over, there they were,
Five little robin eggs.

Keefe Downes (11)
Denton Primary School, Northampton

The Nest

I was gazing at everything,
When I saw it, high in the tree,
A robin's nest with five speckled eggs,
I was so astounded,
I nearly fainted,
The robin's nest in the tree.

Isla Draper (11)
Denton Primary School, Northampton

The Walk

Slowly, as I walk along,
I see the most wonderful thing,
A bird's nest,
Covered in leaves,
With five baby birds,
I note a robin flying free.

Chloe Darvill (11)
Denton Primary School, Northampton

The Horse - Haiku

Across moors it goes,
Like a spirit running free,
At peace with nature.

Emma Payne (11)
Denton Primary School, Northampton

Bright Eyes - Haikus

She is like the night,
Eyes gleam like the brightest stars,
Face glows like the moon.

Cameron Rhodes (11)
Denton Primary School, Northampton

Python · Haiku

The starving python
Stalks its helpless, tasty prey
With fury it strikes.

Charlie Priestman (10)
Denton Primary School, Northampton

Alfie · Haiku

Alfie is my dog
He's always there to greet me,
With his wagging tail.

James Burrow (10)
Denton Primary School, Northampton

Simile Poem

I am as cross as a rhino who
Gets flies on my back,
All my friends have gone away.

I am as happy as an elephant
Luckier than anyone who gets more water and grass.

I am as calm as a monkey with a banana.

I am as happy as a snake who can eat a mouse in one gulp.

I am as sad as my creature who is coming for me.

Oscar Jones (8)
Greens Norton CE Primary School, Towcester

Simile Poem

I am as angry as a fire-breathing dragon
Whose brother broke his moneybox.
I am as angry as an elephant who walked into a wall,
I am as calm as a monkey with bananas,
I am as aggressive as a tiger who can't find his prey,
I am as scared as a meerkat whose predator is coming.

Thomas Atkinson (9)
Greens Norton CE Primary School, Towcester

Simile Poem

I am as angry as a monkey without his banana,
Or having his home taken away from him.

I am as excited as a wolf,
Who has just found the biggest pile of meat ever discovered.

I am as sad as an elephant without a trunk.

I am as scared as a baby taking its first steps.

I am as happy as a squirrel who has the largest
Stash of nuts in the world.

Harry Fleming-Belt (10)
Greens Norton CE Primary School, Towcester

Simile Poem

I am as cross as a monkey because people are eating me
And my best mate.

I am as angry as a lion who has been trapped by the hunters.

I am as sad as a cat whose mum has been killed.

I am as happy as a dog who is going for a day out.

I am as excited as an elephant because I am having a bath.

Joshua Murphy (7)
Greens Norton CE Primary School, Towcester

Simile Poem

I am as angry as a fire-breathing dragon
Who has had his fire extinguished,
I am as angry as a wolf who has eaten an ant,
I am as angry as a lion who has been hunted down,
I am as angry as an elephant who has a knot in his trunk,
I am as angry as a cat who has been bitten by a dog,
I am as angry as a horse who hasn't had any apples.

Ethan Wray (7)
Greens Norton CE Primary School, Towcester

Simile Poem

I am as cross as a cheetah,
Escaping from his predator.
I am as happy as a dragon
Who has burnt down a village.
I am as annoyed as a rhino who has fallen on his back.

Ben Byles (9)
Greens Norton CE Primary School, Towcester

Feelings

I am as angry as a wolf with no meat to eat.
I am as angry as a leopard with no prey to kill.
I am as angry as a hunter with no dead meat.
I am as happy as a kid on his birthday.
I am as sad as a mum whose child has lost his life.

Alexander Ward (8)
Greens Norton CE Primary School, Towcester

Simile Poem

I am as angry as a giraffe with no leaves to eat,
I am as angry as a giraffe with nothing to eat,
I am as happy as a giraffe with lots of food,
I am as angry as a giraffe with no home,
I am as happy as a giraffe with everything I need.

Max Lakin (8)
Greens Norton CE Primary School, Towcester

Happiness

It tastes like ice cream,
It smells like roses,
It looks like a beautiful garden, full of wildlife,
It sounds like birds singing in the trees,
It's multicoloured with green swishy leaves and a clear blue sky.
It feels wet and silky when you walk through it,
Happiness makes me feel great.

Thomas Ashton (9)
Guilsborough CE Primary School, Northampton

Happiness

Happiness is the colour of the sun,
Happiness is eating a whole cream bun,
Happiness is smelling the freshly cut grass,
Happiness is not shouting and being harsh,
Happiness is about sharing,
Happiness is about love and caring,
Happiness is heartfelt fun,
Happiness is a praying nun,
Happiness is the sound of children singing
And the distant noise of church bells ringing,
Happiness feels like a warm glow inside,
Happiness is a feeling I cannot hide.

Emily Ainsworth (10)
Guilsborough CE Primary School, Northampton

Fear Is Like . . .

The smell of petrol and smoke,
The cry of the dead,
The painful screams of a knife
Cutting into soft flesh,
The blood coming from the bath tap,
The black cloak of a murderer next door,
A door being closed,
The rest of your life disappearing,
The room where no one dares to tread,
The mirror steamed up with a man locked inside.
Forget fear and it will leave you.

Aven Dando (9)
Guilsborough CE Primary School, Northampton

Happiness

It tastes like ice cream,
Its colour is light pink,
It smells like flowers,
It looks like a rainbow,
It sounds like birds singing,
It feels like teddies,
It makes me feel great!

Cameron Walker (9)
Guilsborough CE Primary School, Northampton

Happiness

Happiness is yellow,
It tastes like marshmallows in chocolate,
It smells like flowers down a meadow,
It looks like a beautiful ray of sun,
It sounds like children having fun in the street,
It feels like the softness of a cat's fur on my cheek,
I love happiness.

Jessie-Jo Dodd (10)
Guilsborough CE Primary School, Northampton

Sadness

Sadness is grey,
Sadness sounds like a continuous beeping echoing in your ear,
Sadness tastes like cold, hot chocolate,
Sadness looks like a never-ending black space,
Sadness smells like a damp cave,
Sadness feels like a cold starving hand.
Sadness.

Nathan Stroud (10)
Guilsborough CE Primary School, Northampton

Joyful

Joyfulness tastes like sweet strawberries with single cream,
It smells like blossom blooming on the trees,
It looks like joyful children playing in the summer sun,
It sounds like baby birds singing us their song,
It feels like your soft bed covers snuggled all over you.

Joyfulness makes me feel delightful.

Emily Rose Ashmore (10)
Guilsborough CE Primary School, Northampton

Joyful

Joyful tastes like sweet strawberries,
Joyful smells like a BBQ,
Joyful looks like a bright sunset,
Joyful sounds like grateful birds singing a wonderful song,
Joyful feels like a soft teddy,
Joyful makes me feel great.

Taylor Parr (10)
Guilsborough CE Primary School, Northampton

Happiness

The sugar-white clouds floating by,
Ready to journey through the turquoise sky.
The taste of cream and caramel in your mouth.
The sound of baby birds starting to grow.
The smell of spring in the air.
Happiness can be everywhere.

Jumana Mihell-Mufti (10)
Guilsborough CE Primary School, Northampton

Pain

Pain is blood-red,
Pain tastes like chilli curry,
It smells like rotting flesh,
Pain looks like agonising disaster,
The sound of pain is screaming death,
Violence and pain hurt people.

Joe Collins (9)
Guilsborough CE Primary School, Northampton

Happiness

Happiness is turquoise,
It tastes like lollipops,
It smells like sweet red roses,
Happiness looks like sweet little chicks hatching,
It sounds like baby birds chirping in the morning.

Charlotte Cox (9)
Guilsborough CE Primary School, Northampton

The Cheeseburger

The people wait outside McDonald's,
They see the vans driving up the street,
They scream and wave and stand on their feet,
I see them run,
I see them sprint for the cheeseburger,
Some just eat the bun,
Some just eat the cheese,
People like them, I say,
People would eat them all day,
It smells of red sauce, cheese and burger,
It feels warm and refreshing,
It looks like a ball of fire,
It tastes like hot cheese,
The cheeseburger is as bright as the sun,
It sounds like the footsteps crashing with in the rush
To get to McDonald's.

Robert Partridge (10)
Hallbrook Primary School, Leicester

Emotions

Sad is blue like the sky and sea,
Sad is salty water,
Sad is dead flowers,
Sad is a screeching dog.

Happiness is yellow like the sun,
Happiness tastes like fluffy chocolate ice cream,
Happiness smells like flowers,
Happiness feels like soft silk.

Hate is red like pouring blood,
Hate tastes like chilli,
Hate sounds like screaming children,
Hate smells like rotting fruit.

Rebecca Beeching (9)
Hallbrook Primary School, Leicester

Horror

H is for horror like in a spooky house
O is for your own opinions
R is for rescue, when will they come?
R is for fun, running away from fear
O is for options, like getting away fast!
R is for relief, home at last.

Rebbeka Allison (11)
Hallbrook Primary School, Leicester

My Family

M um cooks me delicious food and treats,
Y ummy days out with my family.

F amily are my silver and gold treasure forever,
A t times it can be tough but we stick together,
M y family are the best, no other family can beat them,
I can't wait till we go on holiday together,
L ovely gifts they get me for my birthday,
Y ellow is the bright colourful family.

Emma Rathbone (10)
Hallbrook Primary School, Leicester

The Haunted House

There once lived a boy called Mike,
Who slept in a haunted house at night,
Something went *bang!*
He screamed and ran,
He never went back to see the black cat.

Some days went by,
The haunted house cried,
But Mike never came,
He must have been alright,
But he had had a fright.

Mike came back
Something went *crash!*
'A cat! A cat!'
A sigh of relief, 'it's only a cat!'
So Mike carried on going back,
To visit his grandma.

Emily Turton (10)
Hallbrook Primary School, Leicester

Sweets And Chocolates

Sugar melts on my tongue,
It tickles the back of my throat,
I bit some chocolate, the caramel runs around my mouth,
Sweets and chocolate are happiness,
They look like a sunny beach,
They smell like melting chocolate,
They sound like the most vibrant beat ever,
They taste like melting sherbet,
They feel like soft velvety chews,
Sherbet pours out of its tube,
It sprinkles into a pot,
Kit-kats have to make way,
For the sherbet pot.

Laura Smith (10)
Hallbrook Primary School, Leicester

Bad Feelings

Fear is black,
It smells of saltwater,
It tastes of ink,
It feels like squidgy, slimy, horrible, green slime,
It sounds like a thunderstorm.

Hate is grey,
It smells of rotten eggs,
It tastes of metal,
It feels like crushing somebody extremely close,
It sounds like ghostly footsteps.

Loneliness is brown,
It smells of rotting compost,
It tastes of hot iron,
It feels like a sticky ice cube,
It sounds like a World War II air raid.

Natasha Elks (10)
Hallbrook Primary School, Leicester

The Haunted House

In the haunted house at night,
Everything changes!
In the day it's colourful, happy and bright,
At night it's the complete opposite,
The clocks turn as black as mould,
Tables and chairs come to life!
All the curtains shut
And all the doors open,
So all the ghosts can move around.
All you can hear is the storm outside
And the screams and shouts
And all you see are ghosts and creatures.
You feel very scared.

Katie Hickley (10)
Hallbrook Primary School, Leicester

My Pet Hamster

M y pet hamster is so great
Y ummy treats because she's my mate!

P laying on her wheel through the night,
E very day sleeping snug and tight,
T he way she gives me a hug,

H appily in her den chewing her rug!
A nd she is really cool,
M y dream is to bring her into school,
S o cute in her cage,
T o the scrapbook she's on every page!
E very moment with her is good,
R eally nice cos she's my bud.

Ben Craig (10)
Hallbrook Primary School, Leicester

Haunted House

Bats and blood and slimy goo,
Ghosts that pop out to say, 'Boo!'
Ghouls are fools so are vampires too,
They all come here to scare you.
Witches, wizards, sleek black cats,
Cauldrons, potions just gone crack.
Spells gone wrong, goblins shout,
You hardly ever see these about.
It's my haunted house so stay away,
Unless you want these scary creatures to come and play.

Hannah Edwards (10)
Hallbrook Primary School, Leicester

UFOs

U nknown flying objects glide in the night,
F lying high up, unseen, as if it was a ghost,
O bjects floating over people's houses, silent as a falling leaf,
S peeding like a jet at full speed.

Kieran Brennan (11)
Hallbrook Primary School, Leicester

My Friends

M y friends are Tia, Beth, Ruby, Emma and Hannah,
Y elling to our mates to see Hannah Montana,

F riends are always loving, happy and kind,
R ambling on about nothing but no one seems to mind,
I love all of my helpful friends,
E nemies try to destroy our dens,
N o one ever falls out,
D aydreaming when we're out and about,
S un is shining all day long!

Lauren Mellowes (10)
Hallbrook Primary School, Leicester

In The Middle Of The Ocean

In the middle of the ocean . . .
Fish swirling and twisting,
Like birds in the sky,
Imaginary sea horses charging,
Like bulls across the sea,
Dolphins jumping in and out of the ocean,
Bubbles bubbling underneath the sea,
The waves in the ocean
Are waving at me.

Shannon Samarczuk (10)
Hallbrook Primary School, Leicester

Hairdressers

Hairdressers wash your hair,
Hairdressers like shampoo,
Hairdressers cut hair in layers,
Hairdressers colour new hair,
Snip, trim, wash, comb, dry, brush,
I love my new hairstyle!

Catharine Hewkin (10)
Hallbrook Primary School, Leicester

Fireworks

F ireworks are really cool,
I ndigo, blue, yellow and purple,
R eally, really loud,
E veryone loves them,
W e always go to see them explode,
O r stay at home and watch them in the sky,
R ed, yellow, pink or blue,
K nowing that everyone is safe,
S ee sparkles sparkle down below.

Tia Pullen (10)
Hallbrook Primary School, Leicester

Hate

Hate is red like the Devil of Hell,
It tastes like spicy chilli,
It smells like rotting potatoes,
It looks like green slime,
It sounds like thunder,
It feels like being hit in the stomach.

James Owen (10)
Hallbrook Primary School, Leicester

The Bobbing Balloon

The balloon which my cousin got,
He pinged it all the time,
He usually pinged it to look cool,
Until I got really annoyed,
Like someone had punched me in the face,
So I popped it!
Bang!

Rachel Neal (9)
Hapton VC Primary School, Norwich

Catherine Wheel

Catherine wheel is a twirling firework,
It is a ball of fire,
It is noisy and sparkles,
As it spins round and round,
It gets slower and fainter,
Then it burns out.

George Tuffield (10)
Hapton VC Primary School, Norwich

My Trip To The Roof Of The World

As I take my trip to the Himalayas,
I shiver like an excited dog.
I climb the breath-taking mountain,
Looking for the wilderness I crave.
I can feel the encroaching glacier,
Breaking and cracking under my feet,
As I climb into the foggy clouds.
I see the jet planes fly and eagles in the sky,
Unlikely bed follows, wing tip to wing tip,
As the glacier moves down, I feel claustrophobic,
And I can see the woolly trees,
Almost snugly,
The cold feels folded up to my chin.
At the top of the mountain,
I can hardly breathe.
The view it's amazing,
I can see for miles.
On the way down the slippery mountain,
My face is wreathed in smiles.

Sarah Lomas (11)
Hulland CE Primary School, Ashbourne

Snow Wolves

The atmosphere is desolate,
Shadows are here and some disappear,
Cold wolf tears fall into the bitterness of the ice and snow,
Furry coats offer little protection,
Avalanches of snow are like a million pieces of a chandelier
Shattered and crushed together,
Coughing endlessly the wolves whimper
And stumble into claustrophobic caves.
The wolves den is cosier and warmer than the blistering,
Biting, blizzard on the mountain.
The cubs rub against their mother's chest now warm,
How they love the delicate fur, wavy and long,
A mother's devastating fear of the cubs
Pounding over the sheer cliffs,
As they play contentedly near the edge.
The ice is an electric shock while the wolves hurry
Their paws across the glacier.

Grace Tower (9)
Hulland CE Primary School, Ashbourne

The Yeti

Racing, roaring, ravenous yeti,
White like snow, claws like spaghetti,
I hear crunching snow,
Under crashing feet,
As the yeti approaches hunting for meat,
I am picked up by a huge hand,
Crashing through the forest.
He takes me away,
I thought he may eat me,
This very same day,
But little do I know,
The yeti is kind and eating me
Was the last thing on his mind!

James Rocks (10)
Hulland CE Primary School, Ashbourne

Little Red Turns!

Little Red is a playful one
Funny as a monkey
He's daft, he laughs
And makes me happy
He tickles my toes
Makes me wriggle
At night he makes me giggle.

But sometimes he overreacts
And occasionally attacks
Sometimes he whacks
But I hope he never smacks
My little human friend
Who has no human friends
I am like a dog without a tail
Waiting for the funny one to come back once again.

Bobby West (10)
Hulland CE Primary School, Ashbourne

My Bumpy Ride

A blur of red in front of me,
Fast shadows towering, darkening my thoughts,
Giant hands clutch me,
And I am on its back,
As big as a giant,
With long stringy red fur,
That is warm and soft.
Running now,
We run through the snow,
Ducking, dodging,
Flying like the wind.
My stomach is churning,
My thoughts are whirling,
Abducted.
Alone.

Kerry Redfern (10)
Hulland CE Primary School, Ashbourne

Edelweiss

So white, snow-white,
Petals like silk,
Special like gold.
Tiny white petals blowing in the breeze,
Delicate and bright, shining in the light.
So rare and so fair,
Shining, sparkling, glowing, graceful,
The snow is falling low on the ground,
The wonderful, white winter is upon us,
The sad snow covering me up,
So small and so rare,
Shall I pick it . . . No!

Georgia Parsisson (10)
Hulland CE Primary School, Ashbourne

Mountain

The high view from the wide open spaces,
The beautiful Himalayan landscape,
They seem so quiet, sleeping almost,
Not sleeping though are the yetis,
Furry and shy,
Big cuddly bears,
Looking for warmth,
Wary of the scary grey wolves,
Scavenging for food,
Around Mount Everest table,
Hunting in packs.

Tia Lewis (11)
Hulland CE Primary School, Ashbourne

Snowflakes

Frozen icicles,
White with fright,
Crystal colour,
Shining bright,
Crunchy footsteps,
Spoiling the snow,
Numb fingers as coldness spreads,
Falling snowflakes rushing down,
From white heavens above,
The white wonderland,
Crushed beneath my careless feet.

Emily Redfern (10)
Hulland CE Primary School, Ashbourne

Abducted By Yetis

Stranded as cold as an iceberg,
With my only comfort,
The large looming presence that brought me here.

The rock beneath my feet was crumbling,
I was sure of it,
The yetis were very shy creatures but quite big,
They comforted me and made me feel like
I was on top of the world,
I was on top of the world in my dreams anyway.

Shannon Aggett-Phillips (10)
Hulland CE Primary School, Ashbourne

The Roof Of The World

H imalayas are
I cy, every step you slip, the
M ountains are huge
A nd they are found
L ooming on the border of India
A nd China
Y aks ascending slow and steady
A bove the mountains
S now tumbles down from a cloudy sky.

Liam Hemsil (10)
Hulland CE Primary School, Ashbourne

Red, One Ears And Me

Like a fish out of water babbling confused,
But nice and warm against a wall of red fur
In the snow, cold and alone.
Then surrounded by yetis that started to moan
All blinded and wet
I felt trapped like a fish in a net
I slumped like a lump onto the cave floor
Because my fingers made them numb with frostbite
That were bleeding and raw.

Tiegan Lawson (10)
Hulland CE Primary School, Ashbourne

The Japanese Invasion

Tanks and infantry roll across the border
Like a wave coming up a beach.

Machine guns rip apart the poor defence
Like a wave hitting a sandcastle.

Guns rip apart the barbed wire like hands tearing silk.

When the tanks have gone, we begin our journey.

Mending our hearts and trying to find forgiveness.

William Ripley (11)
Hulland CE Primary School, Ashbourne

The Interloper

A ruined life has been brought here to our secret snow paradise.
The future of our species is fading away,
We have become mortal,
We have a new ruler,
An interloper.
He must be eliminated,
But wait: perhaps he is the Dalai Lama,
Coming to save us from our future?

Claire Wilson (11)
Hulland CE Primary School, Ashbourne

Summer

Summer tastes like ice cream and jelly
Summer sounds like water hitting rocks
Summer smells like barbecues
Summer looks like children having fun
Summer tastes like Coca-Cola
Summer tastes like ice cream
Summer tastes like ice lollies
Summer looks like children playing
Summer sounds like children splashing in the water
Summer smells like fresh air
Summer smells like happiness
Summer tastes like ice cubes
Summer tastes like lemonade
Summer tastes like a jelly
Summer tastes like a KFC
Summer looks like flowers growing
Summer tastes like barbecues.

Connor Wagstaffe (8)
Kensington Junior School, Ilkeston

Trees And Grass

T he grass is long with leaves scattered on the floor
R eally big and really tall
E veryone likes trees
E ven when they are small
S o when you see a tree, know they save the world

A lways save the world
N o trees, no world
D o a good thing for the world

G rass is good
R eally good world with grass
A nd never cut trees down
S how the world your appreciation
S top your dog from digging grass.

Alfie Smith (8)
Kensington Junior School, Ilkeston

Long, Short And Big

The grass is long
The tree is long and red
The shed is long and big
The fence is big and brown
The house is long and brown
The cloud is big and white
The road is long and black
The leaf is small and green
The sky is long and blue
The Devil is short and black
The door is long and red
The rock is long, red and black
The scissors are short and shiny.

Lewis Truman (8)
Kensington Junior School, Ilkeston

Faithful Leap

My sweet little Appiano horse,
Speeds around the jumping course,
He clears each jump with inches to spare,
Cantering round, leaping with care,
Through the finish line, the first round is done,
In the jump-off he'll have to run,
Faster and faster, against the clock,
He came out clear,
We were deafened by the cheer.
My lovely Merlin, he jumps his heart out,
He always comes clear without a doubt.
My little winner.

Bethany Marsden (10)
Kensington Junior School, Ilkeston

Winter

Winter looks like hot dogs,
People having fun in the snow,
People wearing hats and gloves,
People having so much fun,
So much delicious food for everyone.
Winter, winter, so cold and freezing,
Tissues and colds being passed on,
Because snow is so much fun,
Winter smells like fresh air,
People's footsteps in the snow,
Because they're having so much fun,
Winter smells like Christmas dinner.

Alicia Law (8)
Kensington Junior School, Ilkeston

Summer

Summer tastes like ice cream and jelly
Summer smells like bonfires
Summer looks like birds and trees.

Tommy Dennis (8)
Kensington Junior School, Ilkeston

Summer

Summer tastes like ice lollies, ice pops, ice cream
And jelly and ice cream,
Summer looks like the sun and bees,
Opened flowers, sandcastles too,
Summer smells like freshly cut grass,
Also fish and chips and barbecues,
Summer sounds like ice crackling in water,
Lawnmowers and screaming,
Waves crashing, birds singing.
That's what summer's like.

Brooke Cannon (8)
Kensington Junior School, Ilkeston

Winter

Winter looks like snow
Winter looks like people building snowmen
Winter tastes like hot chocolate
Winter tastes like Christmas dinners
Winter sounds like fireworks
Winter sounds like snow crackling
Winter smells like bonfire toffee
Winter smells like Christmas dinner
And winter is so, so brilliant!

Chloe Dickens (8)
Kensington Junior School, Ilkeston

Summer

Summer tastes like jelly and ice cream
Summer tastes like ice lollies
Summer smells like fresh fruit
Summer smells like sandwiches
Summer sounds like children playing
Summer sounds like people slurping drinks
Summer sounds like waves crashing
Summer is absolutely hot and beautiful!

Thomas Law (8)
Kensington Junior School, Ilkeston

66

Winter

Snow, snow, snow is fun when you're out sledging around
Snow fights too
A big snowball too
Make a ginormous snowman
He will come and get you too.

In winter you drink hot chocolate
You have hot dogs too
Sunday dinner too.

Owen Naylor
Kensington Junior School, Ilkeston

Summer

Summer is coming, you know when it's here
Because the birds and the bees will be near.
You can feel it's warm, it might be a bit breezy
You will see all the flowers,
Summer is here, you know that it is
Because of all the ice cream, the chips, the beach,
The fair and the paddling pool,
Summer is here and it rules!

Lauren Wilkinson (8)
Kensington Junior School, Ilkeston

Winter

People playing in the snow with hats and scarves and gloves
People eating hot dogs
Sometimes you see people playing in their homes
With tissues around them because they've got a cold
When you are out sliding, *weeeheee!*
You can smell fire
People running around to keep warm
You can't see any leaves on the trees.

Madison Dean (8)
Kensington Junior School, Ilkeston

Summer

Summer tastes like ice cream
I like summer when it's not a rainy day
And the sun is shining
Summer smells like fresh flowers and freshly cut grass
Summer looks like a baby robin bobbing around,
I love summer!

Jasmine Badder-Walster (7)
Kensington Junior School, Ilkeston

Summer

Summer smells like fresh air
Summer sounds like children playing in the sea
Summer smells like the sun
Summer smells like happiness
Summer tastes like Coca-Cola
Summer sounds like lawn mowers.

Max Henshaw (8)
Kensington Junior School, Ilkeston

Summer

Summer smells like showers
Summer looks like flowers growing
Summer sounds like barbecues
Summer tastes like ice cream with a cone
With a big Flake and chocolate and strawberry sauce.

Milann Bingham (7)
Kensington Junior School, Ilkeston

Parasailing

Parasailing seems very scary
But it is actually quite slow
When you look down you feel quite wary
When you're up, the breeze blows in your face smoothly.

Raj Dhillon (8)
Kensington Junior School, Ilkeston

Summer

Summer tastes like hot chocolate and jelly
Summer smells like chicken legs
Summer sounds like people playing
In the summer it sounds like the trees rustling.

Charlie Barker (7)
Kensington Junior School, Ilkeston

Summer

Summer is so good
You can smell barbecues and freshly cut grass
People build sandcastles
Summer is so good.

Ryan Dickens (7)
Kensington Junior School, Ilkeston

The Sun

The sun was brighter than the glittering stars,
The fire was hot and longer than a trail of blood
The sky was bluer than blue paper.

Reece Purnell (8)
Kensington Junior School, Ilkeston

My Unreal World

In my unreal world I saw . . .

A dog with an upside down head,
I saw a planet sat upon my bed,
I saw some sheep sat inside The Death Star!
I ran for hours but didn't get that far,
I killed the beast that threatened my town,
I gave the gods a reason to frown,
I even stopped the world going round

And . . .

I saw the sound that saw my poem
And saw the things it saw me see.

Bradley Smith (11)
Loscoe CE Primary School, Heanor

At The Seaside

Oh, I love the seaside,
I love playing in the sand,
Watching the waves splash
And listening to the band.

Oh the sand is so white,
It glistens in the sun,
Why don't you come and play with me?
We can all have fun!

Oh, the sea is so blue,
It is so big,
I'm so tired now,
So let us have an ice cream with my friend Stig.

Holly Bourne (9)
Manor House School, Ashby-de-la-Zouch

The Pig

Oink, oink, dirty pig
You really need a wig.

Oink, oink, dirty pig,
Do you want a fig?

Oink, oink, dirty pig,
Why do you want to dig?

Oink, oink, dirty pig,
Do you want to play tig?

Hugo Weir (9)
Manor House School, Ashby-de-la-Zouch

The Sea

I love living
By the seaside
The best thing
In the world
Is playing on
The golden sand
Playing in the
Deep, blue sea.

Isabel Hall (9)
Manor House School, Ashby-de-la-Zouch

Books

I love to read,
It gives me a good feeling,
I would read all day if I could,
Except on Saturdays when I buy books,
I love to read,
It gives me a wonderful feeling,
So I write poems about the 'B' word
And by the way the 'B' word is *book!*

Gabriel Leeming (10)
Manor House School, Ashby-de-la-Zouch

Trains

I love trains, yes I do,
I love trains, how about you?
Some go choo, choo,
The others go beep,
I love trains, do you?

Jonathan Smallshaw (10)
Manor House School, Ashby-de-la-Zouch

The Black Hole

My! What a giant black hole,
It's as big as the North and South Pole,
It's like space jelly,
With images from telly,
With the shape of a baby's bowl.

James Johnson (9)
Manor House School, Ashby-de-la-Zouch

Darkness

The sky's as dark as ever
Animals moving as slow as a snail
Time never moving by
Will fairies save us today
Before we all fade away?

No rivers to keep us alive
What will we do before we die?
The world is falling apart
Will fairies ever come
To save us from this darkness?

The sun is hiding away
Will it ever come out to play?
Please come and save us
Fairies suddenly appear
'Hooray!'
Everyone cheers.

Megan Lynam (10)
Mapperley Primary School, Mapperley Village

Where Does A Black Hole Go?

I said to my mum one Monday morning,
'Where does a black hole go?'
She replied with a sigh and shook her head,
Gave a little mumble, 'Here we go again!'
I thought of the possibilities beyond the hole . . .
A chocolate world,
A green world,
Or just a storage for coal,
I decided to write to Neil Armstrong,
Ask him some questions about space,
He might know, he's been to space,
I wonder what it's like?
Imagine if an alien was there and he asked me to cook
You know what I'd cook him?
A proper English breakfast,
Bacon, eggs and beans,
I asked one more time,
'Where does a black hole go?'
My mum was annoyed, my mum was quite cross,
So she told me to clean out the hamster!

Charlotte Alton (11)
Mapperley Primary School, Mapperley Village

Space - Cinquain

Pitch-black
Comets flying
A rocket from NASA
Here comes a rocket - 3, 2, 1
Blast-off!

Liam Attwood (10)
Mapperley Primary School, Mapperley Village

Light From The Red Planet

I glared graciously at space at the peculiar planets
Wandering through space like a hiker going round in circles.

I stared suspiciously at the scary black sky,
Watching the rocket going to space,
Looking like a glowing beacon in the sky.

I looked longingly into space at Haley's Comet,
Zooming by at tremendous speeds with its lumpy frosty surface.

I hoped hopefully one day I would see the solar eclipse,
Looking like a black orange 10 weeks old.

I cried curiously at space,
Shivering at the soft UFO in my garden,
Pulling me away to a far away place.

Ben Moss (10)
Mapperley Primary School, Mapperley Village

Space · Cinquain

Floating
Gravity low
UFO in vision
5, 4, 3, 2, 1 . . . blast-off! *Woosh!*
Kaboom!

Sophie-Nicolé Bloor (9)
Mapperley Primary School, Mapperley Village

Fairies · Cinquain

Magic,
Fluttering wings,
As small as a blue tit,
Wings like white rose petals that fly,
Magic!

Tia Cooke (11)
Mapperley Primary School, Mapperley Village

Space's Secrets · Cinquain

Darkness
Soaring comets
Golden freckles above
Illuminating satellites
Magic.

Adam Westhead (11)
Mapperley Primary School, Mapperley Village

Unicorn · Cinquain

Crystal
Beautiful horse
Magical unicorn
Colourful unicorn's beauty
Pure white.

Lexy Joan Adams-Shaw (10)
Mapperley Primary School, Mapperley Village

What Am I?

I walk as quiet as a mouse or like rain,
Pitter-pattering in winter,
Paws as warm as melted chocolate,
Heating up in a microwave,
My fur is as soft as a knitted sweater,
Coated in sheep's wool,
First I growl then bark as loud as a firework going off on
                                                    Bonfire Night,
Ears as silky as drapes, just imported from China,
Mouth as wide as an egg yolk,
Just boiled for my breakfast,
My tongue as wet as a freezing puddle in the city,
My smell is as bad as coffee mixed with salt, pepper and vinegar,
Teeth as white as new fallen bits of snow on Christmas Eve,
Steady as a balance beam I am,
My eyes are sparkly as a crystal-blue water fountain.

Daisy Kerry (8)
Millfield Primary School, North Walsham

My Kitten

When she walks, her eyes stare like a dark witch
Brewing up an evil spell,
Her fur is as soft as a royal silk,
The type a king would wear,
She has whiskers as delicate as an antique object,
Hundreds of years old,
The teeth in her mouth are as sharp as a carving knife,
Chopping up meat,
As she walks, her paws pad along the ground like a tiger,
Ready to pounce at its chosen prey,
She has ears as thin as the paper in the Holy Bible,
Only just a bit pinker,
When she hears a random sound,
The silky fur on her head, body and tail prick up.
. . . again as if she was a tiger, ready to jump.

Faye Minton (8)
Millfield Primary School, North Walsham

My Giraffe

I have a long neck, as long as a young tree,
I can reach the leaves from high above.

My long slippery black tongue helps me grab food like a
slippery snake,
A pattern of brown dots camouflage me from danger,
It looks like I have paint thrown on me,
My eyes glitter and I can see very clearly for miles away,
I live in the lovely hot Africa where green trees wave,
My body is soft as silk and as smooth as a new puppy,
I walk with my head up high, very proud but very slow,
My feet are like a horse's hooves,
Clip-clopping along the road, my ears are very soft
And I have a great hearing.

I love to eat vegetables.

Saffron Magnus (9)
Millfield Primary School, North Walsham

What Am I?

A big tongue as sloppy as a dog,
Medium hands but stronger than the Earth.

A cave as dark as anything,
A tail as sharp as a knife,
A strange-shaped body as a bouncy castle
But much bigger and stronger,
Claws as sharp as the sharpest sword in the world,
It eats meat as quick as a fast attack,
Teeth as sharp as razor blades, and as tough,
A nose as big as a massive football but harder,
Ears as big as a fruit bowl and harder,
Feet and legs as big as a four hundred-foot football pitch
And it runs like a jet plane.

Vincent Willard (9)
Millfield Primary School, North Walsham

My Fairy

My fairy's eyes are like the sparkling, shimmering summer light
before dawn

Her footsteps are as quiet as mice eating cheese
And their footsteps too
And my fairy's behaviour will always be as cheeky as me!
As fairies gather round for their summer party,
They are all chatting about how *wonderful* they look
As pretty as loads of pairs of butterfly wings!
Well that's what they think
Their homes are as tiny as my little finger,
They are made out of leaves, wood and bark,
Just like my own bedroom.

Emmie Wright (9)
Millfield Primary School, North Walsham

What Am I?

My ears are as pointy as sharks' teeth,
My fetlocks are as shiny as a new golden key,
My blaze is as white as the swirling snow outside,
My socks are as silver as dolphin's skin,
My feet are as black as onyx shining in the sun,
My eyes are as blue as the very deep sea,
My fur is as gingery as gingerbread,
My tail is like shimmering silk,
What am I?

A horse.

Deanna Christine Harriet Harrison (7)
Millfield Primary School, North Walsham

What Am I?

I look like a cuddly, fluffy cute bear,
My fur feels like a cosy blanket,
You feel warm on a cold, wintry icy day,
I run like a car driving quickly on a bumpy road,
My claws are as sharp as a knife,
My body is as long as a tiny stretcher,
I have a nose that is really twitchy,
My whiskers stick out like a puppet that's just been made,
My body looks like a round circle,
My ears stick up like a dog when it's excited.

Alice Hodson (8)
Millfield Primary School, North Walsham

Dog

Its smell is as strong as a bull far, far away,
Its nose is as cold as ice in a freezer,
Tongue as wet as a puddle in the city lights,
The ears are as pointy as a flower in the countryside,
Its bark as loud as a megaphone.

Jack Wicks (9)
Millfield Primary School, North Walsham

What Am I?

Her paws are as soft as a leather gaming seat,
Her tongue is as rough as wood,
Her teeth are like holly leaves,
She chews into stuff like a panther eating meat,
She scampers across the floor with claws clicking
Like marbles banging together,
She yaps as loud as a drum and her fur is as soft as a silk dress.

What am I?

I am a dog.

Rosie Elizabeth Phillips (8)
Millfield Primary School, North Walsham

My Dolphin

Eyes as shiny as some blue polished glass
A laugh as cold as an ice-cold puddle on a freezing morning
In the bright blue sea, she swims like a dainty dancer in a ballet class
Her fin is as sharp as a needle
Body as soft as a blanket covering a baby in a pram
She catches her food as quick as a flash of lightning in the dark sky
Tail so strong, it pushes her through the waves like a girl
Struggling through a sand storm
Her baby is as tiny as a sparkling crystal in the crystal cove.

Amy Louise Hewitt (9)
Millfield Primary School, North Walsham

What Am I?

My eyes are as bold as a dark, dark city,
My nose is as small as a button worn on a damp cardigan,
My tail is as frizzy and soft as a piece of fluff,
My body is as round as a bumpy oval,
My whiskers are as long as a piece of string that's the size of a ruler,
My walk and bounce are like a see-saw going up and down,
My ears will pop up if I see something exciting,
My fur is as soft as a cat that's rolled in a blanket for the winter.

Harleigh Byers (8)
Millfield Primary School, North Walsham

What Am I?

I live in water, and I am a pet,
My tail is a bit bigger than my body,
I do not have a tongue,
I move in the water, by twisting and turning,
My fins push me along the water,
My eyes can see underwater,
When you touch me, I feel bumpy,
When you see me under the water,
I look as shiny as new gold.

Louise Jane Armitage (8)
Millfield Primary School, North Walsham

Turtle

Her face is as grumpy as an old man,
She walks as slow as a spotty cat,
Her nose is as small as a frosted leaf,
Her skin is as slimy as green goo.

Her body is as rough as a hard rock,
Her shell is as hard as a wooden door,
Her eyes are as bold as owl's eyes,
Her mouth is as small as a patch of green grass.

Bradley Shaw (8)
Millfield Primary School, North Walsham

Monkeys

Their feet are as small as a baby's glove that's first born,
Their eyes are as wide as an A4 piece of paper,
Their ears are as pointy as a blade that has cut off someone's head,
Their fur is as soft as a quilt from the B&B store,
Their teeth are as sharp as a blade that's chopped off
                                        people's heads,
They will eat as many bananas as we have in a week
And stuff the bananas in their mouths like me and Alex do.

Tom Joseph Wardle (9)
Millfield Primary School, North Walsham

Monkey

Its feet are as small as a newborn baby's foot,
Its arms are as long as a snowy street outside,
They will eat as many bananas than you will ever eat in your life,
Its face is as cute as mine and Tom's face,
Its eyes are as wide as a planet floating in space,
Its teeth are as sharp as an executioner's blade,
Ready to chop someone's head off.

Alex Gray (9)
Millfield Primary School, North Walsham

What Am I?

Eyes as bright as a shiny new star in the dark sky,
Nose as smooth as fresh leather on a new sofa,
Her ears pricked up like a thorn on a rosebud, just been picked,
Lives in China in the tall trees as high as Big Ben,
My high-pitched scream is as sharp as a roller coaster,coming to
a halt,
Its fur is as red as blood on a vampire's fang.

Jodie Weller (9)
Millfield Primary School, North Walsham

What Am I?

I can smell food over 10 miles away,
My teeth are as sharp as knives glinting in the light,
I can run faster than lightning when I am catching prey,
My nose is as wet as some raindrops falling in the fresh air,
My fur is softer than silk for a beautiful princess' dress.

Millie Abbs (8)
Millfield Primary School, North Walsham

Ectobog

Like molten metal, hot enough to fry diamonds
As intelligent as a human, clever enough to build a space station
A body like a cup of old, smelly yoghurt
Arms like scaly lizards that are newborn
A tail like an arrowhead.

Daniel Swindells (9)
Millfield Primary School, North Walsham

What Am I?

My eyes are as cute as a newborn baby kitten,
Body as smooth as a new opened rubber,
My beak is as orange as a shiny orange sweet wrapper,
In a new sweet shop in the street.

Elizabeth Skinner (9)
Millfield Primary School, North Walsham

Sammy

Sammy my hamster,
Brown and white,
Lives in a cage,
Comes out at night.

He rattles in his big red wheel
And gobbles up his food,
He loves to climb across his cage
And often has a snooze.

He plays along his ladder
And runs from floor to floor,
The only thing he can't do
Is escape through the door.

He rolls around in his ball
As happy as can be,
I love Sammy
And Sammy loves me!

Jessica Amy Townsend (11)
Rothersthorpe CE Primary School, Northampton

That's The Greyhound

A thin, flamboyant and sleek creature,
Fast as a cheetah,
A bony body and tremendous tail,
The colour fur of a hay bale,
That's the greyhound.

Nothing can stand in its way,
Nothing can keep it at bay,
Rabbits and hares don't have a chance,
Everyone who sees it will be in a trance,
That's the greyhound.

Even hunters can't get this prize,
It doesn't matter about their size,
Compared to this creature,
Its wonderful features,
Because of its slender shape,
It will always escape,
That's the greyhound.

As its wonderful life begins to end,
Its tail and legs start to bend,
But it will keep running,
Running, running,
Until it drifts up into the air,
And has another life there,
Now that's the greyhound,
Forever.

Madeleine Aber (9)
Rothersthorpe CE Primary School, Northampton

The Starfish

In the misty waters, a starfish lay,
Underneath the gravel, he catches his prey,
The sticky starfish swims away,
Never to be seen after that day.

Amber Smith (10)
Rothersthorpe CE Primary School, Northampton

My Friend

I have a friend,
He makes me laugh,
Nearly every day,
But one day he lost his 'funny'
And had nothing to say.

Lots of days went past,
But no one ever dared to laugh,
He lost his mojo,
He was not cool,
He lost his will to play the fool.

Every day I would wait, but nothing,
Until one day when I heard, something,
I wandered over to see who it was,
And it was a bunch of people laughing
Because . . .
He was there and so was his 'funny'
Standing in the playground, where it was sunny.

How did he get it back?
We're not really sure,
Perhaps he pulled some from his backpack,
Or . . . he'd been out, and brought some more?

No one will ever know!

Ella Wellington (11)
Rothersthorpe CE Primary School, Northampton

The Airport

The airport is like a busy ant's nest,
The airliner sometimes flies east or west,
The airliner flies like a fussy bird,
The airliner is like a silver rocket,
Up,
Up,
Up in the sky is a silver plane.

Max Stilp (9)
Rothersthorpe CE Primary School, Northampton

The Snake

So amazing is the snake,
Moving soil in its wake,
You pick it up and you've been tricked,
As slowly the snake starts to constrict,
Suddenly you have a fright,
When the snake gives a deadly bite,
Then the bite starts to poison you,
You have no idea what to do,
You really haven't got a clue,
The constriction is stopping your breath too,
In a while you will be dead,
Then an idea pops into your head,
You pick up a rat from the floor,
Boa wants you no more,
Instead it grabs the rat,
And lets you go just like that,
Then you start to feel OK,
As the poison fades away,
But Boa suddenly sees he's been tricked,
And grabs you again and starts to constrict.

Luke Townsend (10)
Rothersthorpe CE Primary School, Northampton

The Dog

There was a dog
Who lived in a bog
He found a stone
He thought it was a bone
And went to bury it.

He dug a hole
And found a mole
Then he scurried around
Then he found a tunnel
Which was shaped like a funnel
And nobody saw the dog again.

Benjamin Walker (11)
Rothersthorpe CE Primary School, Northampton

Phantom Of The Socks

I do like my grandma,
But not her taste in socks,
She bought me bright orange ones,
Bright orange ones with polka dots!

I tried flushing them down the loo,
Putting them in the bin too,
They keep on coming back.

I threw them out of the upstairs window,
I even fed them to our dog, Bingo,
They keep on coming back.

I sucked them up the vacuum cleaner,
I was mean but they were meaner,
They keep on coming back.

I chucked them in the local river,
I put them in a pig's liver,
They're out to get me,
Phantom of the socks.

Ashlyn Hope Ricketts (10)
Rothersthorpe CE Primary School, Northampton

Battle

A king and queen at both sides,
Knights with swords ready to stride,
Pawns will be the ones sent in first
And many need the attending of a nurse.

Bishops using magic like never before,
Knights and horses breaking down the door,
The king and queen are in peril,
As an army is ready for war.

The queen tries to defend her man,
But she too must bow down,
The king closes his eyes and awaits his fate,
As they hear a cry, 'Check mate!'

Michael Herd (11)
Rothersthorpe CE Primary School, Northampton

86

Imagine A World

Imagine a world with blue grass,
Imagine student exams always with a pass,
Imagine a farmer who doesn't have a cow,
Imagine when you walked in a room everyone had to bow.

Imagine a world where the moon was an apple,
Imagine a Jacuzzi in a chapel,
Imagine ants begging on the streets,
Imagine Hallowe'en with tricks and no treats.

Imagine a world where school was fun,
Imagine the North Pole had sun,
Imagine scarecrows with a roar,
Imagine America without a tour.

Imagine a world where boys wash,
Imagine a storm where raindrops don't splosh,
Imagine Britney Spears as a vet,
You would prefer this world I bet!

Charlotte Guerin (10)
Rothersthorpe CE Primary School, Northampton

Mad Misty

My hamster, Misty, is as mad as can be,
Sitting upon the wheel,
Rolling in the sawdust trying to clean.

Misty is mad,
Pebbles is calm,
But worst of all Freddy is young and scared.
Taking Freddy out is a real challenge,
Trapping him here and there,
He always manages to escape.

Pebbles is always asleep,
She is never playing on her wheel.
Misty is always on her wheel,
Never is she sleeping.

Danielle Louise Smart (10)
Rothersthorpe CE Primary School, Northampton

In The Playground

The bell rings,
Playtime begins,
Suddenly a fight has begun,
As all the teachers run,
The children watch,
The fight carries on,
'Oh please Miss he kicked the wall'
'No - I - never, I kicked the ball.'
'Even worse you made a hole in the wall!'
'That wasn't me, that was the ball.'
'Both of you just get inside,
While I find out the story - then I'll decide.'
The bell rings,
As playtime ends,
They grab their pens
And get back to work again.
Silence!

Francesca Partridge (10)
Rothersthorpe CE Primary School, Northampton

Camping Weather

Water plopping on my head,
It's raining once again,
Gather up the cases
And all aboard the train.
Arriving at the campsite,
I spot the weathervane,
Things are looking pretty bad,
Next time let's go to Spain.

Joshua Leonard (9)
Rothersthorpe CE Primary School, Northampton

The Superhero Poem

Little Joe thought he was a superhero,
But all his friends called him a super zero,
He wore his pants inside out
And from his mum he got a shout,
He wore some boots and a cape,
They were held together with sticky tape,
He called himself Ultraman,
Although he didn't have a single fan,
He dreamt of being in comic book heaven,
Even though he was only seven,
He had a U on his shirt
And his arch enemy was Bully Bert,
Little Joe said he could teleport,
His dad said, 'Of course you can,' but that's not what he thought,
His parents shattered his dreams,
Of having super beams.

Thomas Ross Coleman (10)
Rothersthorpe CE Primary School, Northampton

Dogs

Dogs sometimes are very friendly and kind,
They like to eat whatever they can find,
You can pet and tame them,
You can even name them,
They'll be a friend for life,
Especially in times of strife.

Wild dogs are very mean,
They're usually quite thin and lean,
They sometimes live in their very own den,
Their enemy is men,
They look mainly for food,
They also can pick up on your mood.

Dogs that are pets are man's best friend.
The end!

Bethan Jade Wesley (10)
Rothersthorpe CE Primary School, Northampton

YoungWriters

Tongue Twisting

At school we did some tongue twisters
(Gave my tongue a couple of blisters)
Everyone was singing fine,
While I couldn't even keep in time,
Still everyone can talk a lot,
But my tongue is stuck in a knot!

James Daman (11)
Rothersthorpe CE Primary School, Northampton

In The Staff Room

In the staff room the teachers eat,
The teachers talk, the teachers sleep,
In the staff room the teachers chat,
The teachers shout, the teachers sit on big brown cats!
In come the children one by one,
Out come the teachers for the classroom run!

Abigail Kate Ashby (11)
Rothersthorpe CE Primary School, Northampton

Droids

Good ones,
Bad ones,
Battle ones,
Repair ones.

Strong ones,
Weak ones,
Jedi ones,
Sith ones,
Ones for good,
Ones for bad.

Lots of models,
Lots of units,
Lots and lots of Droids.

James Tinnon (10)
St Botolph's CE Primary School, Peterborough

Dragons Big, Dragons Small

Dragons big, dragons small,
Dragons thin, dragons tall,
Red and yellow, blue and green,
All the dragons are really mean,
Flying through the sky at night,
Giving people such a fright,
Gobbling people up with chips,
Burgers, pizza, pies and kips,
Kiddies for pudding, maybe more,
Babies, grown-ups, food galore,
Before they're eaten, cows go moo,
Chinese dragons are long and slim,
Eating people by the chin,
Teeth turn yellow, black and gold,
At a wedding there's a party crasher,
It's a dragon named Masher.

Rrrroooaaaarrrr!

'Argh, oh no, there's a dragon down the road!
Run, hide, cos there's a dragon coming!'

Thomas Allen (10)
St Botolph's CE Primary School, Peterborough

Lost

Lost in the desert,
Lost in the sea,
Lost in the jungle,
Look at me!

Looking about,
Holding my weapons,
Getting them ready,
To go *bang, bang,*
Bang!

Francesca Errico (9)
St Botolph's CE Primary School, Peterborough

War

People are screaming,
Running for shelter,
Bombs are dropping,
Buildings are falling.

Soldiers attacking,
Guns at the ready,
Lambs to the slaughter,
Screaming with pain,
War's not a game.

Medics are working,
Stitching up wounds,
Soldiers are dying,
Last wishes told.

Unwanted telegram,
Mother's dread,
Families feeling the pain,
War's not a game.

Sam Johnson (10)
St Botolph's CE Primary School, Peterborough

Seasons

Summer, autumn, winter, spring,
One by one the seasons go,
Everybody having fun,
Meeting people as they run.

Summer is the time for fun,
Everybody playing,
People eating yummy cakes,
People playing in the lakes.

Winter is a time for cold,
People are in their house,
Playing with their teddy mouse,
Having no fun.

Jessica Driscoll (10)
St Botolph's CE Primary School, Peterborough

Wipe Out!

Everyone is wiped out
Death is world wide
This is not a war Sir
This is genocide
Bomb shelters are running out
Torpedoes above our heads
Nobody can run away
So hide under your beds
Do what you can
Hide in your hall
Build barriers around your house
Or just end it all.

Daniel Hill (10)
St Botolph's CE Primary School, Peterborough

Prowling Predator

Crouching in the long grass,
Waiting to pounce,
Claws digging into skin,
Food for the pride.

Curious cats,
Cubs running to their king,
Jumping and playing, chasing a tail,
Dozing in the sun,
Sleeping next to their mum.

Sarah Brett (10)
St Botolph's CE Primary School, Peterborough

War

War is bad
War is dangerous
War is sad
War is mad.

Adnan Khan (9)
St Botolph's CE Primary School, Peterborough

Aliens

Brain like a nut
Tail like a blade
Black like leather
Blood of acid
Faster than a car
Teeth like knives
Hands like heads
Run fast, run quick
They're after you.

Stephen Coupland (10)
St Botolph's CE Primary School, Peterborough

Dragons

Dragons they fly, they take to the sky,
Well there's a surprise, they're dragons,
What do they do? Fly in the blue, that's very, very true.

So what do you do when you see a dragon?
You stay very still!
Dragons are small, dragons are tall,
Red eyes, blue eyes,
All different in size.

Lewis Baldwin (9)
St Botolph's CE Primary School, Peterborough

Kittens

Kittens are smart,
They like to play,
They are so cute,
Except in the litterbox tray.

Kittens are funny,
Like any other cat,
This is the bad part,
When they kill rats.

Tia Briers (9)
St Botolph's CE Primary School, Peterborough

Sweets

S ave the world, it's the only planet with chocolate,
W ater melon isn't as good as Dolly Mixtures
   or a gobstopper or two,
E very child has to try one including me and you,
E ven if you're old or young, go on have a go,
T wo sweets are better than one but don't get greedy,
S o hope you enjoyed this poem, I did.

William Pierce (9)
St Botolph's CE Primary School, Peterborough

World War II

Bang, bang,
Bombs dropping on the houses of London.

Bang, bang,
Guns firing at soldiers in battle.

Bang, bang!

Kane Popay (9)
St Botolph's CE Primary School, Peterborough

Parks

In a dark, dark park
There was a dark, dark car
And in the dark, dark car
Girls were screaming like mad!

Sebastian Roberts (10)
St Botolph's CE Primary School, Peterborough

Flowers

Flowers, flowers, start to grow,
First you must sprinkle water,
To make them grow beautiful and nice,
To dance in the rain.

Daisy Eisler (10)
St Botolph's CE Primary School, Peterborough

The Gulf

A gulf of wonder
A gulf of mysteries
A sea of excitement
A rumble of thunder.

A gulf of mysteries
A hot bath
A rumble of thunder
As clear as glass.

A hot bath
The waves begin
As clear as glass
Even Mum went in!

The waves begin
What could be in there?
Even Mum went in
Up comes a fin.

What could be in there?
I don't know
Up comes a fin
What I do know though
This is the gulf of Mexico.

Thunder and lightning
A sea of excitement
Up comes a fin
A gulf of wonder.

Benjamin Luck (11)
St Nicholas House School, North Walsham

A Dog Named Paris

Sparkling eyes,
Fluffy coat,
Sharp teeth,
Pointy ears.

Fluffy coat,
Pointy ears,
Cute bunches,
Sparkling eyes.

Pointy ears,
Sparkling eyes,
Cute bunches,
Tiny bark.

Little princess,
Tiny bark,
Lots of licks,
Climbs over and under.

Little princess,
Lots of licks,
Climbs over or under,
Irresistibly sweet.

Irresistibly sweet,
Climbs over or under,
Little princess,
Sparkling eyes.

Georgie Ryan (10)
St Nicholas House School, North Walsham

Smoky

A little rebel,
A furry ball,
An energetic soul,
A small hamster.

A furry ball,
He's a monkey,
A small hamster,
A climbing frame.

He's a monkey,
He's a cloud,
A climbing frame,
As grey as grey.

He's a cloud,
He can do monkey bars,
As grey as grey,
His fur is soft.

He can do monkey bars,
His sweet little ears,
His soft fur,
His tiny eyes.

A furry ball,
His name is Smoke,
A small hamster,
He's all mine!

Helen Frances Rose Little (10)
St Nicholas House School, North Walsham

Minky Whales

A black shape,
Lurking in the water,
Small water volcano,
Comes out of the water.

Lurking in the water,
Something black,
Small water volcanoes,
Big fin comes out of the water.

Something black,
On top of the sea,
Big fin comes out of the water,
Goes, then comes back.

On top of the water,
Swims round the boats,
Goes then comes back,
Big, small and in between.

Swims round the boats,
Making strange noises,
Big, small and in between,
Here, there and everywhere.

Making strange noises,
Comes out of the ocean,
A minky whale,
Lurking in the water.

Sam Hicks (11)
St Nicholas House School, North Walsham

Alfy

A ginger kitten
A little devil
Here comes Alfy
The kitten rebel!

A little devil
Who scratches me!
The kitten rebel
Here comes Alfy!

He scratches me
And fights with the dog
Here comes Alfy
Watch out for that mog!

He fights with the dog
And makes Mum mad
Watch out for that mog
Because he is super bad.

He makes Mum mad
That ginger kitten
He is super bad
Here comes Alfy, the kitten!

Flora Gair (11)
St Nicholas House School, North Walsham

Tennis

Opponents, singles, doubles,
Bounce the ball, serve the ball, *wham!*
Win the point, lose the point,
Bounce the ball, serve the ball, *wham!*
The umpire shouts out the score,
Bounce the ball, serve the ball, *ace!*

Ben Alger (10)
St Nicholas House School, North Walsham

Dolphins

Cold waves,
Clear as crystal,
Dolphins jump,
Swim over to me.

Clear as crystal,
The dolphins swim,
Swim over to me,
By my feet.

The dolphins swim,
Around me, by me,
By my feet,
I feel the ripples of the ocean.

Around me, by me,
I feel their playfulness,
I feel the ripples of the ocean,
I see the beautiful coast of New Zealand.

I see the beautiful coast of New Zealand,
Cold waves,
Clear as crystal,
I feel the spray of the salty sea.

Abigail Lawrence (10)
St Nicholas House School, North Walsham

It's There

It's hot up there,
It's cold down there,
I don't know what to say.

It's green there,
It's blue there,
I can't tell which to compare.

It's so hard,
To compare or say,
So I'm going away.

Ethan Moreton (11)
St Winefride's Catholic Primary School, Shepshed

The Demon Dentist

Today's the day - hip hip hooray,
I wish to say - I love the dentist,
His beady eyes, evil hands,
My brother whispering in my ear,
'The demon dentist, the demon dentist.'

Entering the waiting room,
My legs like jelly, arms shivering,
Dread, fear, helplessness,
My brother whispering in my ear,
'The demon dentist, the demon dentist.'

I hear them cackle my second name,
It's our turn now, please can we go home?
About to push open the door,
My brother's whispering in my ear,
'The demon dentist, the demon dentist.'

I lie down on the chair,
Not half bad, 'Comfy' I say,
I have to open my mouth - uh oh,
My brother whispering in my ear,
'The demon dentist, the demon dentist.'

Phew - it's all over now,
I don't believe I was so scared,
Although my brother had to have:
2 fillings,
4 teeth out,
6 holes - I could go on,
He's not whispering anymore!

Jemima Briggs (11)
St Winefride's Catholic Primary School, Shepshed

Summer Holiday

The final bell rings,
'At last' I say,
'Here comes the summer holiday,
I cannot wait to start anew,
Although there is some homework I need to do,
I wonder what I'll do next year,
Secondary school: number one fear!
But I shall not worry,
Till that time comes,
No more *homework,* no more *sums!*'

When I get home,
I flick on the TV,
Whilst I eat fish and chips for a lovely tea,
Then comes a really late night,
Try if you might,
But I shall not sleep!

I love a morning lie in,
I sleep in until 11 o'clock,
I wake up to the sight of last week's smelly socks!
My friends are coming round for dinner,
Sweets, chocolates, I'm not getting thinner,
I'm enjoying my holiday.

Erin Hull (11)
St Winefride's Catholic Primary School, Shepshed

Random

As red as the sun,
As green as the pears,
That might be
Why I can't compare.

Worms are slimy,
Worms are cool . . .
The reason why I like them so,
Because they're full of fuel!

Thomas Laxton (11)
St Winefride's Catholic Primary School, Shepshed

My Dreamland

I had a dream last night,
A magical one too,
I dreamt about a dreamland,
Yellow, green, red and blue.

I dreamt about a unicorn,
Perched on its head was a shimmering horn,
I dreamt about the bluebirds
And the little sparrows just born.

I dreamt about the landscape,
Blue mountains clouded with mist,
Fairies danced under rainbow trees,
Oh! I have an endless list!

I dreamt about the animals,
Foxes, rabbits, squirrels and deer,
The blue oceans were full of sea life,
If only it were like that back here!

And so my dream went on,
Throughout the night,
I woke to the sound of my alarm clock,
A Saturday morning's golden light.

Georgia Lowe (11)
St Winefride's Catholic Primary School, Shepshed

Celebrities

Simon Cowell showing off his white teeth
To Katie Price and Peter Andre,
Victoria Beckham is back from her shopping trip
And is having a chat with Cheryl Cole,
Louie Walsh is giving Kylie singing lessons,
Take That are taking up baking,
Torvill and Dean are now on 'Strictly Come Dancing',
Fern and Reggie now do a new show called 'Only in Japan'.
To top it off, the Queen has been to Primark to get a few bargains.

Megan Allard (11)
St Winefride's Catholic Primary School, Shepshed

Rocket Ride

I'd love to go on a spaceship,
All the things I could do,
I'd run with the aliens
And watch the cow jump over the moon.

The rocket would whoosh through the planets,
Mars, Jupiter and Saturn,
Being careful not to bump into the sun,
Or I might turn into an atom.

I'd make friends with an alien
And call it Whippy Woo!
We'd play for hours and hours,
What other things could we do?

Next I'd watch the stars go by,
Wish on every one that flew,
I tried to catch some a few times
And then I heard a *moo!*

I watched the cow jump over the moon
As I went back home again,
Jumped out of the spaceship, happy as could be,
I can't wait for my next ride.

Lucie Cripps (11)
St Winefride's Catholic Primary School, Shepshed

The Colour Of Red

Red is the colour of Liverpool,
Red is the colour of a juicy, bright red apple,
Red is the colour of Man U winning trophies.

Red is the colour of Liverpool fans over at the pub,
Red is the colour of love,
Love is the colour of the heart,
The heart is the place for romance,
Red is for Liverpool.

Lucy Cartwright (11)
St Winefride's Catholic Primary School, Shepshed

I Think The World Hates Me!

I think the world hates me,
I never get a chance,
To show the world I'm a better boy
And it seems to nick my pants.

In class I try my best at science,
Maths and English too,
The world really hates me
And there's nothing I can do.

In PE, it's rounders,
I bet I'm awful at that,
At lunch I found a hamburger
And now guess what? I'm fat.

At break I have to play football,
What a rubbish game
And because I'm rubbish at football,
They all said I was lame.

It's hometime now,
What a relief,
But I still think,
That the world hates me!

Dominic Skeoch (11)
St Winefride's Catholic Primary School, Shepshed

Imaginary

Shiny dragons slayed by a knight,
Fire-breathing dragons, really what a sight,
A beautiful world out in the night,
The moon shining bright, like a guiding light.

Wizards and witches,
When a spell goes wrong,
They put you in stitches.

Kira Louise Rouse (11)
St Winefride's Catholic Primary School, Shepshed

Princesses

Here's a little poem,
About what every girl dreams to be,
When I'm alone at night,
A princess I dream I'll be.

In 'Beauty and the Beast'
They fall in love when eyes first meet,
There's a dancing tea set
And a pretty garden too,
To finish it off, there's a candle that doesn't have a clue.

In Aladdin there is a man who calls his monkey Abu,
He sits and smells others' shoes,
To finish this off there's a flying carpet
And everyone says *woo hoo!*

In Ariel, down under the sea,
A human she will later be,
A dancing crab, a singing fish,
Oozits and Wozits, now make a wish.

Lois Wilkinson (11)
St Winefride's Catholic Primary School, Shepshed

Treats

Oh Daddy, when you go out,
Daddy what do you find?
Oh Daddy are there big ones?
Daddy do they mind?

You come home late every night,
Daddy where do you go?
Oh Daddy, I do wish,
You'd find me a big pogo.

What happens if you come home,
With nothing left to find,
Oh Daddy please answer me,
Or I will lose my mind!

Charlie Heimes (11)
St Winefride's Catholic Primary School, Shepshed

Stupid Mouse!

My favourite colour is blue
And my name is Sue,
I have a big house,
Plus a stupid mouse!
It runs around
Without making a sound!

I have a pound,
Which we've just found,
But my stupid mouse stole it!
My mouse is a hypocrite,
It told me not to steal!
So instead it bought a seal,
Now I'm annoyed.
I need to buy a Druid,
To get that stupid mouse,
Oh no, I think it's run off to kiss our dinner lady,
Mrs Rouse!

William Grant (11)
St Winefride's Catholic Primary School, Shepshed

I Want, I'm Scared

I want to win this contest,
I want to win this game,
I want to win all the cash,
I want to win my fame.

I want to win all this because my friends beg,
I want to win this or they'll break my leg,
It's not fair when they pull my hair,
It's not fair because they are always there,
Just to hurt me,
It's not fair.

All I want to do is hit them with a flare.

Jack Bearpark (11)
St Winefride's Catholic Primary School, Shepshed

The Ice Cream Factory

In the ice cream factory,
Ice cream is being made,
There it goes twisting and turning,
While making a squelching noise,
Like you are walking in wet mud.

The ice cream tasters
Get a shock of cold ice cream,
It is cold as the Antarctic.

When the ice cream is out in the shops,
Children rush in and out,
Buying ice cream and shouting,
We love ice cream.

Ice cream,
A delicious thing,
Always ready to cool you down,
Ice cream is a wonderful thing.

Sarah Cochrane (11)
St Winefride's Catholic Primary School, Shepshed

Dragons

Dragons, dragons, what a sight,
Here and there, that's alright,
Here comes the knight,
That's not alright,
Down goes the dragon,
What a fright.

They fall from the sky,
They should just try to fly
But still they fall.

The dragons lie dead on the floor,
Still, the knight attacks no more.

Joshua Alan Carpmail (11)
St Winefride's Catholic Primary School, Shepshed

109

Wet Playtime

Susan's got rid of the books,
Jasper has tied up the cooks!
Billy and Jack are betting money,
And Tom is trying to be funny.

Alex is hanging off the light,
Lucie and Erin are having a fight,
Aimee is locked outside,
Mrs Rouse has just been pied!

Julian is spraying water,
What's happened to Mr Jones' daughter?
Jasmine is playing with paint,
It's making the teacher faint.

Whenever it's wet at playtime,
Forget adding, Romans and rhyme,
It's just chaos and fun
And always making the teachers run!

Nicola Northcott (11)
St Winefride's Catholic Primary School, Shepshed

School

No school today,
I could watch TV,
I could go out and play,
Or watch the new DVD.

I could sleep all day long,
I could count my cash,
I could sing a song,
Or go to a birthday bash.

'Get up it's school.'
'Aw, Mum!'

Bethany Minskip (11)
St Winefride's Catholic Primary School, Shepshed

My Monster Friend

My little green friend lives under the stairs,
He's not very big at all,
He's really mischievous and very interesting,
But strangely he's never heard of *football!*

My little green friend lives under the stairs,
He loves my army soldiers and my plane,
Whenever I look I can't find them,
To be honest, he's driving me insane!

My little green friend lives under the stairs,
He is friendly, I must say
But if you start playing a game,
He is sure to start to play!

My little green friend lives under the stairs,
He's not very big at all,
He's really mischievous and very interesting,
But strangely he's never heard of *football!*

Alan Cox (10)
St Winefride's Catholic Primary School, Shepshed

Noises Of War

People are crying,
People dying,
People screaming,
All that I can hear,
Is - *bang*, like a massive explosion,
You smell horrible like never before
And there's nothing left.

People walking,
People running,
What's going on?

Callum Marshall (11)
St Winefride's Catholic Primary School, Shepshed

My Dog Follows Me

My dog follows me everywhere I go,
It follows me upstairs,
It follows me down,
It follows me to the living room.

Why does my dog follow me everywhere I go?
It follows me to the garden,
It follows me everywhere,
Even when I go to my room.

My dog follows me everywhere I go,
It also follows me to our conservatory,
It follows me to the kitchen,
Why does it follow me?
Oh yeah,
I know why - because I stroke it everywhere I go,
So that's why it follows me,
I love my dog now!

Billy Harding (11)
St Winefride's Catholic Primary School, Shepshed

Snails

Snails are slimy,
Snails are cool,
Snails have eyes that pop out,
Snails have shells on their back,
Some are yellow,
Some are grey,
But my favourite is purple.

Charlie McManus (10)
St Winefride's Catholic Primary School, Shepshed

Poetry Explorers 2009 - The East & East Midlands

Treacherous Timeline

Who came first?
Egyptians, Tudors, Greeks or Romans?
Well let's find out!

First of all there were the Egyptians,
They were mean and lean and mummified.

Next were the Greeks so great,
They built a horse, a giant horse.

Then there were the Romans,
They ripped animals apart,
Argh!

Now we're at the end
And have reached the Tudors,
If you stirred up a crime in Tudor times,
Your head would be on a spike!

Jonathan Carpenter (9)
Sacred Heart Catholic School, Loughborough

My Family

My family is great,
My daddy's my best mate.
My mummy loves to cook,
While my brother likes playing in muck.
My sister loves to draw,
Whereas I play some more.
My popa has a study,
He sometimes gets muddy.
My grammy also cooks
And likes to read books.
What a great family I have.

Ingrid Guest (9)
Sacred Heart Catholic School, Loughborough

Mitten

I bought a kitten
And called it Mitten,
He grew really big
And looks like he's wearing a wig!
He now has big paws
And very sharp claws,
Huge teeth
And eats beef,
I changed his name to Brian
Because he is a lion!

Izzy Fairbairn (9)
Sacred Heart Catholic School, Loughborough

Guess What It Is?

River-hogger
Special-swimmer
Water-lover
Mother-loser
Furry-cheaper
Lion-hater
Warm-eater
Bird-diver
Mother-finder.

Amber Sharman (9)
Sacred Heart Catholic School, Loughborough

My Dreamland

My dreamland is great,
How I want it to be,
I can go anywhere, even under the sea!
I can change it every day,
Into this, that, anyway!
It's magical and mystical,
It's a real dream come true
And maybe it will come to you.

Elena King (9)
Sacred Heart Catholic School, Loughborough

Teacher

Good helper
Super writer
Sometimes failure
Road rager
Fast typer
Massive winner
Stupid organiser
Nice helper.

Sebastian Spooner (8)
Sacred Heart Catholic School, Loughborough

The Date

One day we went out for a date,
But sadly we were late,
Powly tripped over her dress,
Oh boy she made a mess,
When we had tea,
She spat on me,
Then we left the date,
That I did hate.

Megan Murphy (8)
Sacred Heart Catholic School, Loughborough

Devil

Devil in the sky
Flying in the night
Killing people with all his might
When he's red it means he's in bed
When he's hot it means he's rock
Devil in the bright
Licking lollies with all his might.

Joe Hoy (9)
Sacred Heart Catholic School, Loughborough

My Cat Rosy

My cat Rosy is very nosy,
She always has a bath and splashes around,
She's very puffy and always fluffy,
She always hides when I'm asleep,
I never know where she has gone,
She's bad and always mad.

Zoya Ivanova (9)
Sacred Heart Catholic School, Loughborough

My Rhyming Poem

There is a young girl from Long Whatton,
Whose dog pulled her down on her bottom,
It wasn't a joke,
For her arm, it was broke,
It's something she's never forgotten.

Fiona Whelband (9)
Sacred Heart Catholic School, Loughborough

The Sea

Turquoise,
Leaf-green,
Silvery white horses, overlapping the sand,
Sunny yellow colours of the sun's reflection,
Lavender,
Sky-blue,
The navy-blue sea crashing into the rocks.

Calm,
Raging,
Thrashing the cliffs and beaches,
The sea violent and powerful,
Gliding,
Whistling,
Raging overlapping waves.

William Thompson (9)
Scalford CE Primary School, Melton Mowbray

What Am I?

What am I?
Sometimes I'm blue, sky-blue,
With waves crashing together
And at the top, diamonds, silver,
What am I?
I can be turquoise, pearl or emerald,
Sometimes I'm indigo, jade, metallic or fox-fur brown,
I can be sapphire, violet or bronze,
What am I?
I can sometimes be beautiful,
But then not always, but my colours are amazing,
What am I?
Sometimes I can be a little fidgety,
I can be attacking, dangerous, endless,
Exploding, fast, lapping and powerful,
What am I?
Slippy, sneaky, spiteful, striking,
I can be vast, gushing, lurching,
Also, roaring, scuttling and wiggly,
What am I?
But I am not always violent,
I can be calm and slow,
I can be so peaceful and brilliant,
What am I?
When the sun shines on me,
I shine back, sometimes I'm friendly,
What am I?
I am the sea.

Phoebe Copeman (10)
Scalford CE Primary School, Melton Mowbray

The Sea

The colour of sea
Emerald green, sapphire blue,
Indigo, lilac, mauve too.
Crystal clear, baby blue,
They all make the raging sea.
As waves come in with foam on top,
Crashing against the metallic rocks.
It's full of life, deep inside,
Dangerous, playful and most of all fun.
It unravels the colours every day,
Emerald green, sapphire blue, indigo, lilac, mauve too.

The sea
The sea, the sea
And its many moods,
As calm as a summer's day,
Or more angry than the Devil.
The sea, the sea,
Lapping at your feet like a lively puppy
Or as rough as a bully,
The sea, the sea,
As sneaky as me,
Or more mischievous than Noah.

Milo Burgoine-Roth (11)
Scalford CE Primary School, Melton Mowbray

The Sea

The calm sea sits still,
But as I look again I see
It crashing and smashing
And suddenly it trashing,
Strikes, its anger comes in an immense wave!
This is how I see the sea.

Toby Heseltine (9)
Scalford CE Primary School, Melton Mowbray

Memories

I woke up early one morning,
I crept to the garage,
To see the bike I got at Christmas,
To find that there was an empty garage,
With no bike,
It had been stolen.

The next Christmas,
I got a new motorbike,
And from then on,
I got more and more,
Built up to 4 bikes in the garage,
With 3 up the garden.

I was nervous,
I was scared,
For this special motorbiking day,
It was cold,
Wet,
But when I think of my old bike
I still get upset.

Andrew Hallam (11)
Scalford CE Primary School, Melton Mowbray

The Sea

Lapping, calm, thrashing, swaying,
The calm sea weaving from side to side.
The water on the beach slapping the rocks,
The cockles buried in the sand,
The water cracking them.
Whispering, raging sea, that can be calm and vile!

Red, blue, orange and green,
It can also be rather clean,
The water can be calm,
You can have your beach next to a farm,
Emerald and lime are also fine.

Hannah Perez (9)
Scalford CE Primary School, Melton Mowbray

The Sea

When I looked at the sea,
I saw a lovely sky blue
And when I looked deeper,
I saw some glistening specks of diamonds in the sun,
A few moments later,
I saw a sapphire colour,
Then I saw a powder blue colour, near the edge.

The sea can have many moods,
It can be calm and relaxing,
Or it can be unforgiving,
On some days it can be brilliant,
But on other days,
It can feel like it's endless,
Sometimes it's sliding,
And some days it's crackling,
But we all know it's the sea.

Andrew Truett (10)
Scalford CE Primary School, Melton Mowbray

The Sea

Light, turquoise, bluey-green,
The kind of sandy colour you get in a scene,
Sky-blue waves crashing at the seaside,
We will go and see what there is
And where we could go,
Waves all wavy, coming to us,
We are all getting wet and all damp,
Now the waves are creeping up on us.

Voices
The calm waves whishing and washing the sand away,
Whispering,
When it wipes the sand, leaving wavy patterns,
It explodes on the rocks,
It breaks rocks into little sand bits.

Cara Haywood (9)
Scalford CE Primary School, Melton Mowbray

The Sea

The sea, the sea,
Can go pea-green,
The sea, the sea,
Can turn turquoise,
The sea, the sea,
Can sparkle in the sun.
Bronze, indigo, even jade,
These are the colours of the sea,
The sea, the sea,
Sliding in and out.
The sea, the sea,
Sometimes calm, sometimes not.
Brilliant, mischievous, even powerful,
This is what the sea does.

Hattie Toon (8)
Scalford CE Primary School, Melton Mowbray

The Sea

The aqua waves rippling over my feet,
Olive-green crashes into turquoise,
Emerald and sapphire flowing, they meet,
The sun shines on the maroon-lit sea,
Gracefully and peacefully it will flow,
The beautiful sea, it has a mind of its own.

The sea peaceful and gentle,
It relaxes and calms me,
The sea horrid and mental,
Thrashing and crashing at the rocks so tough,
The smashed rocks left scattered and rough,
The sea, sentimental, it scares me and
Relaxes me, that's what it means to me.

Laura Jackson (11)
Scalford CE Primary School, Melton Mowbray

The Sea

Roaring, roaring, now the sea is mardy,
Roaring, roaring, now the sea is aqua,
Splashing, splashing, now the sea is angry,
Splashing, splashing, now the sea is khaki,
Wavy, wavy, now the sea is turquoise,
Wavy, wavy, now the sea is calm,
Bumpy, bumpy, now the sea is jade,
Tickly, tickly, now the sea is happy,
Tickly, tickly, now the sea is cobalt,
Freaky, freaky, now the sea is tired,
Freaky, freaky, now the sea is a diamond,
Roaring, splashing, wavy, bumpy, tickly, freaky,
Now the sea is everything.

Henry Gyorvari (10)
Scalford CE Primary School, Melton Mowbray

The Sea

The sea, the aqua colour it holds,
Moves when the sea is rough and crashing everywhere,
Jade green, the colour of the coral beneath,
Turquoise, a sea somewhat different,
Like it's in your dream,
Sky blue can be so many colours but still pretty.
Baby-blue, so light, the colour of the sea when nearly see through.
Lurching like an old man's back.
Monstrous like the most evil thing you've ever seen.
The sea is so powerful, left, right and centre.
Endless length, it goes on forever,
Forever more the sea will crash.
Forever more the sea will smash around the rocks.

Charlotte Arno (9)
Scalford CE Primary School, Melton Mowbray

The Sea

Sometimes is turquoise, lovely and blue,
Sometimes leaf-green,
Sometimes fox-fur brown,
Sometimes pearl-grey,
Sometimes navy-blue,
The sea
Roaring and crashing about,
When it's in a moody way,
Shrieking and lurching everywhere,
Calm and leaping over waves,
Never will it stop again.

Amelia Bown-Bhandal (8)
Scalford CE Primary School, Melton Mowbray

Memories

All my memories are good, bad and middle,
They all seem good, but some are bad,
This is a good one, let's hear,
I was playing on a game named Halo 3,
I loved the banshee and the elephant too.
Now here is a bad one,
I was going down the drive
On a scooter, I fell off, scrape, scrape, scrape,
Lots of blood I just couldn't describe.
Here is a middle one, I was climbing a tree
And you could not see me.

Finlay Wright (10)
Scalford CE Primary School, Melton Mowbray

Desert

It sounds like the wind blowing against a house,
Its colour is yellow like a bright sun,
It reminds me of a twirling sandstorm,
It tastes of sandy sandwiches,
It looks like people screaming.

Matthew Foster (7)
Stanwick CP School, Wellingborough

Desert

Desert is the colour of sand, like big rocks,
Desert sounds like the sea's big waves,
It tastes of ice cream,
Like chocolate, vanilla and choc chip ice cream,
It looks like everyone is poor,
Like they have no water,
It feels so hot, like you are touching the sun,
It reminds me of the past,
Like the best things I have done,
It feels like your dry skin.

Lucy Irons (8)
Stanwick CP School, Wellingborough

Lakes

A lake is green with blue in it,
To be just like the sky when it's about to rain,
A lake sounds like the wind at a steady pace,
A lake tastes bitter and cold,
Cold and bitter just like the sea,
A lake looks shiny, glittery and calm,
A lake feels like a smooth piece of wood glittering in the sunlight,
A lake reminds me of the seaside when everyone's playing
And laughing under the sun.

Emma Brown (8)
Stanwick CP School, Wellingborough

The Park

The park is multicoloured,
Like a rainbow in the sky.
It sounds like the wind zooming past,
It tastes like ice cream melting in the sun,
It looks like a rainbow on the ground,
It feels smooth like a tabletop!
It reminds me of playing on my bike,
It smells of laughter coming from the children.

Holly Burroughs (8)
Stanwick CP School, Wellingborough

Haunted House

A haunted house must be the colour black
With bright white eyes all around,
A haunted house sounds like
Every lion roaring angrily,
A haunted house tastes like burnt crispy sausage,
A haunted house looks like a prize given out as you've been there,
A haunted house feels like you've been eaten by a monster,
A haunted house reminds me of a nightmare of people killing me,
A haunted house smells of horrible curry.

Charlotte Irons (8)
Stanwick CP School, Wellingborough

The Lake

A lake reminds me of my grandad going fishing,
A lake is blue like an empty sky,
A lake looks like a gigantic swimming pool
That hasn't been cleaned for days,
A lake sounds like a dog barking,
A lake tastes like dirty water,
A lake feels like a lovely hot day,
A lake smells of picnic food.

Hannah Sutton (8)
Stanwick CP School, Wellingborough

Haunted House

It is as black as the sky,
With a bright green mouth,
With sea-coloured windows,
It smells like dirt rising in the air,
It reminds me of magic,
It tastes like dirt,
It looks scary,
It feels like wood burning.

Courtney Noble (8)
Stanwick CP School, Wellingborough

Danger

Anger is black like a dark and dangerous cave,
It sounds like people shouting out you're in danger,
It tastes like there's danger inside the food,
It looks like there's all traps inside the cave,
It feels like a dangerous animal trying to bite me,
It reminds me of when I went into a cave,
It smells of dangerous things coming towards me.

Ewan Leggate (8)
Stanwick CP School, Wellingborough

Silence

Silence is blue without any sound,
Silence sounds like the winter breeze,
Silence tastes like mushy and horrible food,
It looks like a silent town full of sadness,
It feels really sad and gloomy,
It reminds me of a quiet Victorian school,
Silence smells horrid.

Ruby Paul (7)
Stanwick CP School, Wellingborough

Haunted House

A haunted house is purple and grey like a grey ghost,
It sounds creepy like a monster is behind you,
It tastes like witches' poison with a bit of magic,
It looks like a big purple, broken house,
It feels so scary that you are shaking,
It reminds me of very scary movies,
It also makes me scared.

Harry Stanton (8)
Stanwick CP School, Wellingborough

Desert

A desert is like an orange poster,
It sounds like a gorilla humming to itself,
It tastes like yellow potatoes,
It looks like an orange snake coming towards you,
It feels like a scaly snake,
It smells like a dangerous river,
It reminds me of an old, spooky, sandy palace.

James Heaton-Jones (7)
Stanwick CP School, Wellingborough

Hate

Hate feels like the rage of a gorilla screaming and shouting,
Hate's colour is white like a great white shark,
Hate sounds like the roar of a T-Rex,
Hate tastes like a burning house,
Hate looks like an erupting volcano,
Hate smells like burning food,
Hate reminds me of what someone has done to you.

Zachary Martin-Sinclair (8)
Stanwick CP School, Wellingborough

Garden

A garden's colour is green, like the bush in my garden,
A garden makes me feel smiley and calm,
Like when I see my mummy,
A garden looks like a nice, peaceful place, just like my house,
A garden looks like a nice juicy strawberry melting down my throat,
A garden smells like water splashing on my face,
A garden reminds me of the sunset.

Amy Delauney (8)
Stanwick CP School, Wellingborough

Lake

Lake is blue like our uniform,
It sounds calm and silent,
It tastes of fresh air and cold water,
It looks like a sunny day with a lake in middle and plants around it,
It feels refreshing,
It reminds me of Virginia Waters,
It smells like eating minted Polos on the bench.

Georgia Hilson (8)
Stanwick CP School, Wellingborough

Joy

Joy is multicoloured, like a rainbow and
People bursting with laughter like a clown has visited them.

It tastes like your favourite food.

It looks like a sparkling rainbow.

Joy feels like a party is going on.

George Valentine (8)
Stanwick CP School, Wellingborough

Darkness

The colour is black with a dash of blue in it.

It tastes like lots of insects creeping round and round,
In and out of the fire.

It reminds me of ghosts flowing in the dark.

It feels like I'm in a graveyard with smashing and bashing inside.

Faith Burrill (8)
Stanwick CP School, Wellingborough

A Poem Of Silence

Silence is like a wall blocking information,
Silence sounds like silence,
Silence tastes like something bitter stopping you from talking,
It smells like something nasty,
It looks like a wall,
It reminds me of a lightning strike.

Rory Vartanian (8)
Stanwick CP School, Wellingborough

The Lake

The lake is the colour of the sky
And the sky is the colour of blue,
It feels like smooth rocks and a leaf,
It sounds like a waterfall,
It tastes like tap water,
It reminds me of tears.

Joshua Dawson (7)
Stanwick CP School, Wellingborough

Mountains

It smells cold with a breeze wrapping round my legs,
It's the colour white, like the snow falling to the ground,
It tastes like salt, all sugary and more,
It reminds me of snowdrops at the beginning of spring,
It sounds like rain pattering on the windowpane,
It looks like snow falling on your toes.

Natasha Blakemore (8)
Stanwick CP School, Wellingborough

Haunted House

It is black like a dark night,
It is like a dark sky,
It is like a dark empty book,
It sounds like creaking up the stairs.

Raven Herd (7)
Stanwick CP School, Wellingborough

Excitement

Excitement sparkles like the sun's rays,
Excitement sounds like the waves by the beach,
Excitement tastes like chocolate milkshake,
Excitement looks like the lovely blue sky,
Excitement reminds me of the new bright flowers.

India Wells (7)
Stanwick CP School, Wellingborough

Sadness

It looks like tears down your cheek,
It sounds like crying,
It tastes like teardrops,
It reminds me of people crying,
It's windy and cold weather.

Kyle Francis (8)
Stanwick CP School, Wellingborough

Sadness

It feels like a hard rock,
It is the colour of a grey cloud,
It looks like the rain running down your face,
It tastes like something sour,
It reminds me of a wet and cold day.

Elise Hodge (8)
Stanwick CP School, Wellingborough

Sadness

It tastes like rainwater,
It smells like nothing,
Sadness is black and dark,
It sounds like the fury of the animals,
It reminds me of crying.

Robbie Wilkin (7)
Stanwick CP School, Wellingborough

Lucy's Dream

I took Lucy to bed that night,
Dad couldn't cope,
He hadn't seen Mum for over 20 years.

Lucy fell asleep,
She saw Mum,
She was shining like a star,
She was running towards Lucy
As slow as a moon walk.

Mum was jumping high,
Like on a trampoline,
She was as hot as a cooker,
Lucy felt as happy as a bunny,
Lucy looked like a big ball of fire with happiness.

But then Mum disappeared,
Lucy tried to open her eyes but she couldn't,
Then she opened them and Mum wasn't there.

Tia-Mae Muller (8)
The Grange School, Daventry

Bedtime

You know when most children are asleep,
I'm not!
Do you want to know why?
As soon as Mum is downstairs,
Like all mums are, watching TV,
Me and my brother are tickling each other,
Stealing teddies and messing about.
And at the same time Mum came up and shouted,
'What are you doing at this time of night?'
And we were pretending to be asleep,
Next time she is banning our games and it's still bright outside,
In the morning before Mum and Dad wake up,
We mess about and become their alarm clock.

Alexander Ross (8)
The Grange School, Daventry

Alien Experiment

A liens are as green as grass
L ooking around as dark as night
I t's as bumpy as a Toffee Crisp
E xperimenting with what aliens eat
N eil Armstrong was the first man to step on the moon

E dwin 'Buzz' Aldrin was the pilot
X ylophones are much more colourful than aliens
P urpose, it's only an alien on the moon
E xperimenting with what aliens eat
R ockets on Earth and on the moon
I t smells like mint
M en on the moon
E xperimenting if the moon is made out of cheese
N onsense, the moon isn't made out of cheese
T hey're bringing aliens back to Earth.

Travis Berrill (8)
The Grange School, Daventry

Please Mrs Jumper
(Based on 'Please Mrs Butler' by Alan Ahlberg)

'Please Mrs Jumper, this girl, Lucy-Loa,
Keeps smacking me.
Miss, what shall I do?'
'Go and sit in the window dear,
Go and sit in the bin,
Take your book under a tree, my love,
Do whatever you think!'

'Please Mrs Jumper, this girl, Lucy-Loa,
Keeps ripping my pages, Miss what shall I do?
'Go and sit in the basement dear, move away from her love,
Do what you think best.'

Siân Thom (7)
The Grange School, Daventry

My Friend, Susy!

My friend, Susy,
Smells like a flower!
Looks like a flower!
In fact, she is a flower,
But the only weird thing about her is,
She looks like a human,
In fact I think she is a flower-type human,
And every day she grows bigger, bigger and bigger,
If you think about it, it's really weird isn't it?
Anyway it's a mystery.

Megan Hemmings (8)
The Grange School, Daventry

Spaceships

S pace, there is no rain
P adlock, there are no padlocks in space
A corns, there are no acorns
C heese, the moon is not made of cheese
E mpty, the moon is, space is not empty
S creaming there is no screaming in space
H amster, there's no hamsters in space
I nk, there is no ink in space
P ulling there is no pulling in space.

Louis Hardwick (8)
The Grange School, Daventry

Rocket

R ead a book about space
O uter space is so vast that it can't be measured
C an the moon landing ever happen again?
K ings can't rule the moon
E lectricity helps the rocket fly
T he moon orbits the Earth.

Hassan Jailan (8)
The Grange School, Daventry

Spaceship

S aw a spaceship, it was very big
P erhaps the aliens were staring at us
A ll shaking, on the way to Planet Earth
C an you just hop on the moon?
E verybody was jumping out of the spaceship
S uper duper and off we go!
H ealthy aliens we saw
I saw a green snotty alien
P eople were scared, everybody saw aliens.

Nicole Gilbert (8)
The Grange School, Daventry

Rocket

R ocket steps leading to the moon,
O bjects like rocks,
C old place,
K eep on moving,
E xperiment on the alien,
T ask: to get to the moon.

Fiónn Doherty (7)
The Grange School, Daventry

Rocket

R ough and rocky, such a delight,
O verhead we see the Earth,
C over our heads as the stones fall,
K eep your masks over your mouth,
E at your sandwiches,
T est the craters.

Bethany Macmillan (7)
The Grange School, Daventry

Rocket

R ead books about space
O pen the doors of the rocket
C limb the stairs of the rocket
K eep the doors shut
E at food on the rocket
T ill the rocket lands.

Aidan Landen (8)
The Grange School, Daventry

Make-Up

Make-up can be very pretty,
However it is such a pity,
Animal parts could be in there,
Maybe even a wild hare.

Make-up might look good on you,
But think what a chimpanzee would do,
Blusher you might think is very nice,
However it could be made from little mice.

Silk is made from a silkworm,
But they should not disappear in turn,
When you go to buy a jazzy top,
Make sure you're not going to make a bird hop.

So look for a rabbit sign
And all the animals will be fine.

Hannah Draper (10)
Viscount Beaumonts CE Primary School, Coalville

Cruelty To Animals

Animals are taken away from their homes and habitats,
They end up in zoos and circuses and locked up in cages too,
Their fur is made into clothes for fashion but it would
                                    suit them better than us,
We kill some animals just for their tusks,
It's not fair - why not do it to us?

I would be upset if it was me taken from my home and family,
No home, no food, no water, so can't you understand or see?

It is cruel to be taken away from the people you love
And not be treated properly,
People making you do things you don't want to do.

But even worse - imagine if it was you.

Tegyn Rhosyn Stallard-Higgs (9)
Viscount Beaumonts CE Primary School, Coalville

Anger And Rage

A rguments can decide
N evertheless, you can't decide,
G irls and boys around the world,
E ncourage us to do some good,
R age can control us, don't worry it won't hurt you.

A nimals are cute as well as rare,
N evertheless don't kill them,
D eath can control us, don't worry, it won't hurt you.

R ubbish around the street,
A s well as the beach,
G etting to animals not just us,
E ncouragement can control us, don't worry, it won't hurt you.

Josh Barnes (11)
Viscount Beaumonts CE Primary School, Coalville

A Poem About Pigs

We people kill pigs
Just so we can eat.
Why don't we wait until they are dead
Instead of killing them through the head?
We eat pork chops for lunch,
Munch, munch, munch.
Crackling also comes from a pig,
So why don't we eat vegetables that we dig?
Why don't we eat less,
Instead of making a mess?

Holly Treen (11)
Viscount Beaumonts CE Primary School, Coalville

A Leopard's Skin

People kill leopards just for their skin,
For towels, coats and carpets,
They use their heads as statues,
The same with lions, tigers and bears,
It's very upsetting, they should be free,
Not on the wall in front of me.

Bethan Rose McLeavy (10)
Viscount Beaumonts CE Primary School, Coalville

The Minotaur

The monster is the Minotaur,
He's strong and very bold,
You'll never ever see one,
As they're thousands of years old.

The Minotaur is vicious,
Its growl is deep and loud,
He can scare you on your own,
Or if you're in a crowd.

Isabelle Graham (9)
Waltham on the Wolds CE Primary School

Cyclops - Cinquains

One eye
Eats poor humans
It's smelly, grotesque and
It smells of raw mouldy meat
Beware!

His cave
Is full of lumps
Of white human body
Contents and other disgusting
Items.

One eye
Eats poor humans
It's smelly, grotesque and
Smells of raw mouldy meat
Beware!

Humans
Beware! Smells you
From ten to twenty miles
Run away more than twenty miles
Shoo, shoo.

One eye
Eats poor humans
It's smelly, grotesque and
It smells of raw mouldy meat,
Beware!

Huge as
Nine large buses
He's as brown as can be
Clanks like hundreds of elephants
Wow, loud!

Christopher Morgan-Smith (10)
Waltham on the Wolds CE Primary School

Medusa

Stone turning
Snake-headed
Evil eyes
Scary smile
Snakes slithering
Slimy scales
Shouting, screaming
Scary Gorgon.

Sam Harris (8)
Waltham on the Wolds CE Primary School

Young Writers Information

We hope you have enjoyed reading this book - and that you will continue to enjoy it in the coming years.

If you like reading and writing poetry drop us a line, or give us a call, and we'll send you a free information pack.

Alternatively if you would like to order further copies of this book or any of our other titles, then please give us a call or log onto our website at www.youngwriters.co.uk.

Young Writers Information
Remus House
Coltsfoot Drive
Peterborough
PE2 9JX
(01733) 890066